Revisiting the Classics

Photography and Text
by Don McCunn

Design Enterprises of San Francisco

ISBN: 978-0-932538-75-8
Library of Congress Control Number: 2012941559

Design Enterprises of San Francisco
1007 Castro Street, San Francisco, CA 94114
www.deofsf.com

For prints or framed and matted photographs, visit:
www.Wild-Side-Photography.com

Available to the trade from Ingram Book Company

Acknowledgments

Were it not for the art of the masters, this book would not exist. Models, past and present, have inspired artists through the ages, and my muses include Alexandra Matthew, Jain Dowe, Fallon Niedzwiecki, and Bella, as well as those who prefer to remain unnamed. I am grateful to them and to Alan for bringing together models and photographers.

My work has benefited from the guidance of Bob Elvin, Grant Rusk, and Dave Christensen at the Harvey Milk Photo Center; Sita Bhaumik and Ann Jasper at the RayKo Photo Center. Roxanne Worthington's classes and sharp critical eye in private consultations have been particularly helpful.

Feeling somewhat alone in my exploration of photography as theatre, I am deeply grateful to Layna White of SFMOMA who, on seeing my work, suggested I look at Cindy Sherman's. What a relief it was to then read Sherman's recollection: "When I was starting my stuff I felt completely isolated from traditional photography. I felt like an outcast, not just from the photography world but even the art world,...".*

I appreciate the opportunities Judy Tan and Raymond Tan have afforded me through solo shows at Castro Tarts. I also wish to thank Jay Schaefer for helping me formulate my ideas; Georgi and Archie Blake for their generous support of my work; and Lynda D. Preston for her keen editorial eye.

Above all, I am indebted to my wife, Ruthanne Lum McCunn, for her support and the incisive, creative criticism she applies to all my work.

* "Cindy Sherman," *Vanity Fair*, March 2012, page 385.

Table of Contents

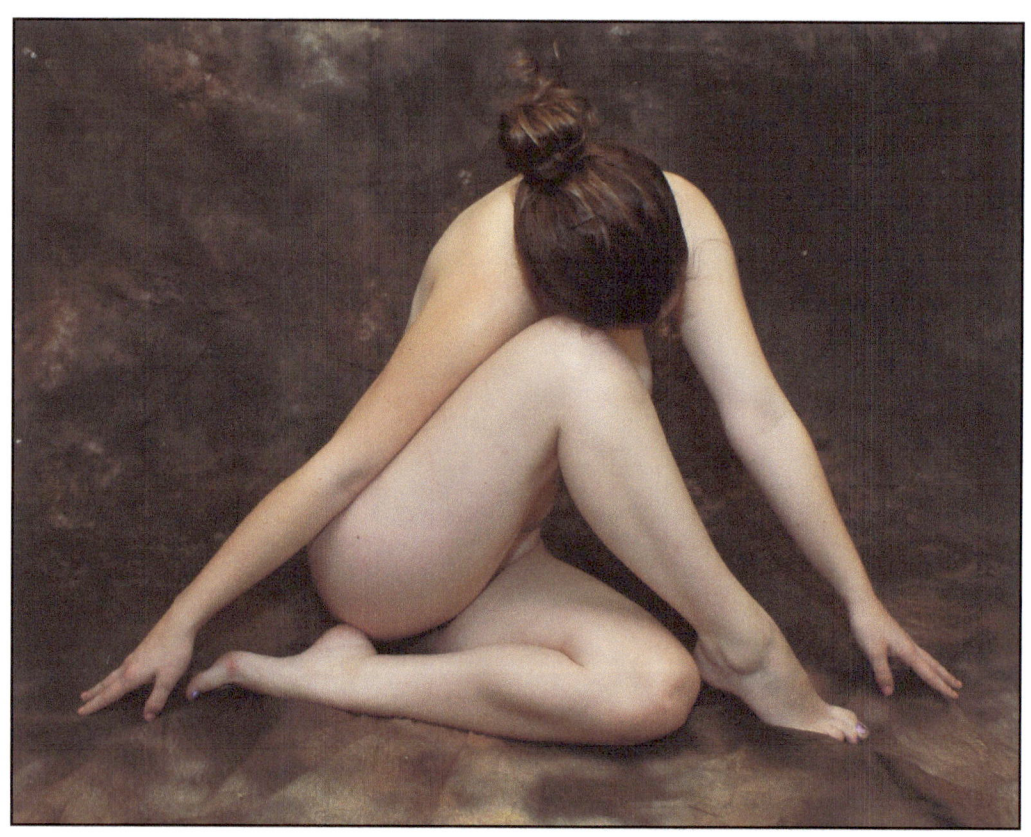

Figure Study #1
Inspired by *Nude 1936*,
Edward Weston, 1886-1958

Introduction

My interest in photography springs from my lifelong passion and experiences in theatre, collaboration with other artists, inspiration from the classics, and the infinite continuum of the creative process.

I began revisiting the classics by sharing Edward Weston's *Nude 1936* with a model who assumed hundreds of variations on the pose, including *Figure Study #1*. Then, by changing the gender of the models, as in Jacques-Louis David's *The Death of Marat*, I offered the story of *The Other Marat*. Exploring the critical role of body language in conveying meaning, I directed the model posing for Édouard Manet's *Luncheon on the Grass* to face the picnickers, rather than away, turning the image into *The Conversation*.

These forays led me to combine poses from different works of art, and I inserted Michelangelo's statue of *David* into Osmar Schindler's *David and Goliath*, creating *The Last Laugh*. I also replicated many classics with live models in homage to their enduring inspiration, which deepened my appreciation of their creators' genius.

Adventuring further, yet following time-honored tradition, I started using the art of masters as touchstones for original work.

Sharing my discoveries on these pages and at my website, Wild-Side-Photography.com, is another step in the journey.

Enjoy!

Don McCunn

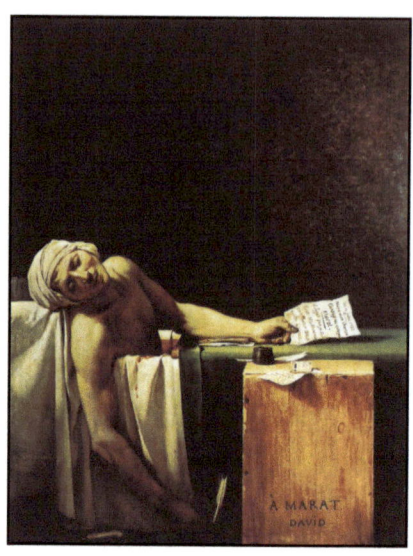

Death of Marat, 1793, Jacques-Louis David, 1748-1825

The subject of this painting, Jean-Paul Marat, was a radical journalist and politician during the French Revolution. Suffering violent itching from a skin disease he probably contracted while hiding in the sewers of Paris, he frequently sought the comfort of a cold bath, and he laid a board across the tub to serve as his desk.

Marat was writing at this desk when Charlotte Corday called on the pretext of giving him information about his enemies' activities. Over his wife's worried protests, Marat admitted Corday, who thrust a five-inch kitchen knife into his chest. Within minutes, he died from massive bleeding.

In memorializing his friend's death, the artist chose to leave out the women and portrayed the knife lying on the floor instead of in Marat's chest. There is also no blood.

The Other Marat considers the fate of his wife.

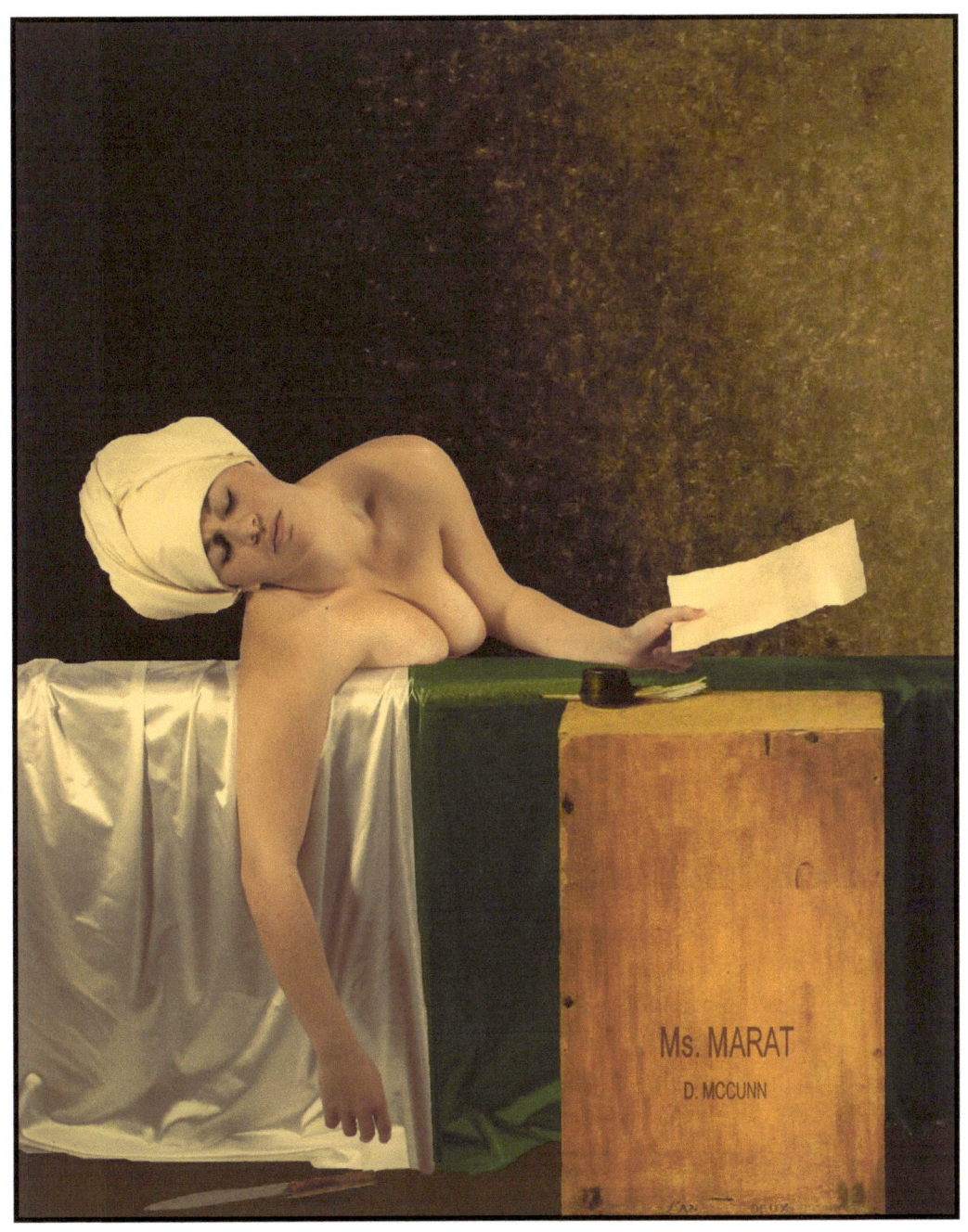

The Other Marat

9

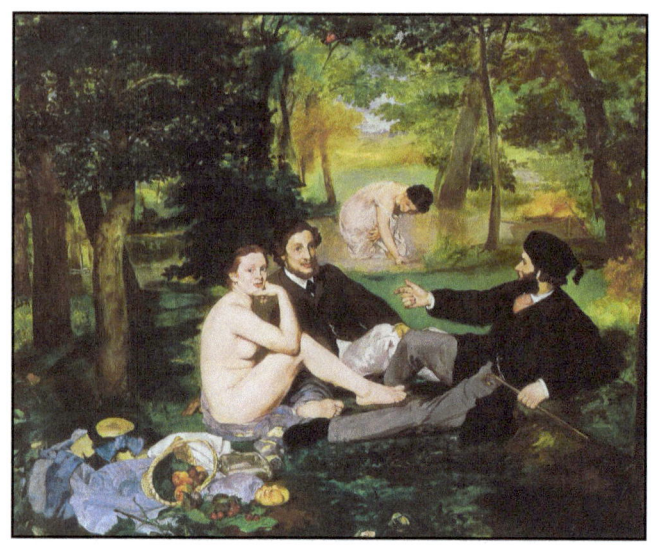

Luncheon on the Grass, 1863, Édouard Manet, 1832-1883

   In painting an unclothed woman gazing at the viewer, Édouard Manet was rebelling against the tradition of nude figures modeled on historical, mythical, or biblical themes.
   When the Paris Salon of 1863 refused to accept the painting, Manet submitted it to the Paris Salon des Refusés. Even displayed in a salon for rejected work, however, the painting sparked controversy and engendered public notoriety.
   The woman in the painting is a combination of Madame Manet's body and the face of Victorine Meurent, who later established herself as an artist in her own right, becoming a member of the Société des Artistes Français.
   Meurent was the inspiration for *The Conversation* in which the woman is an active participant.

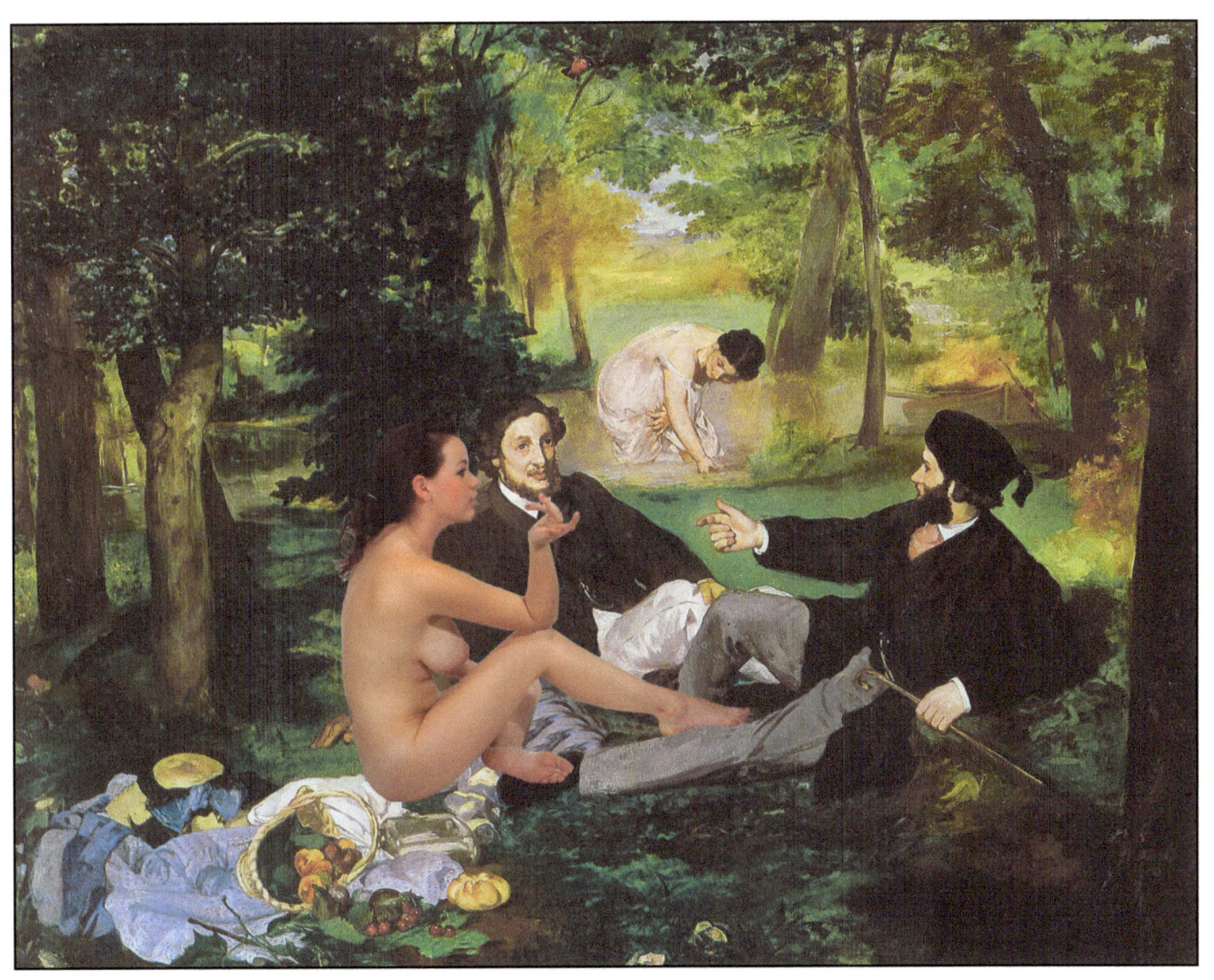

The Conversation

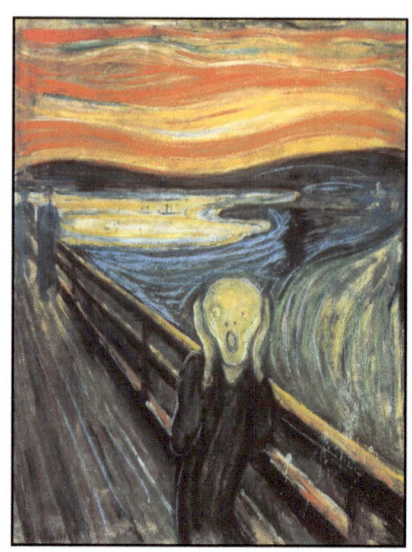

The Scream, 1893, Edvard Munch, 1863-1944

Edvard Munch's diary reveals his inspiration for *The Scream*: "I was walking along a path with two friends—the sun was setting—suddenly the sky turned blood red—I paused, feeling exhausted, and leaned on the fence—there was blood and tongues of fire above the blue-black fjord and the city—my friends walked on, and I stood there trembling with anxiety—and I sensed an infinite scream passing through nature."

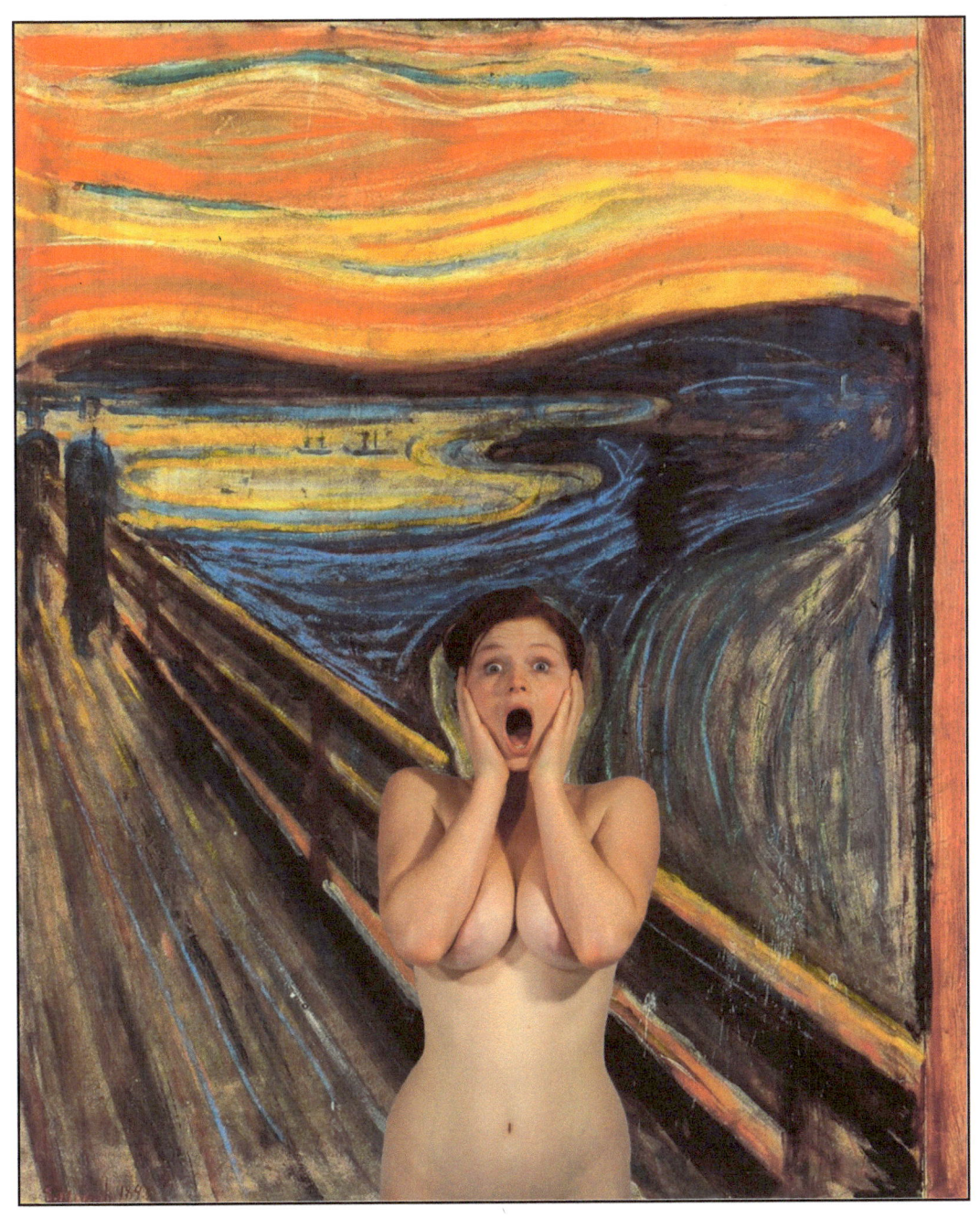

Dreamscape

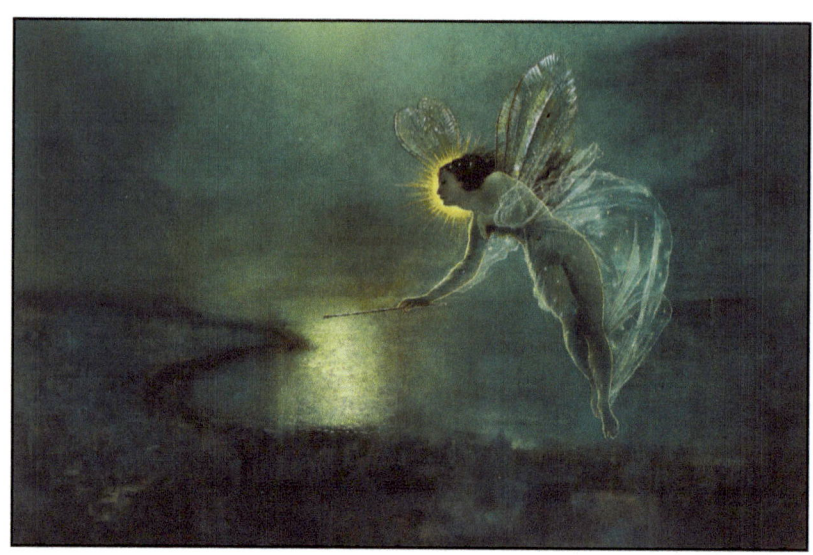

Spirit of the Night, 1879, John Atkinson Grimshaw, 1863-1893

In his twenty-fourth year, John Atkinson Grimshaw quit his job as a clerk for the Great Northern Railway to pursue his passion: painting.

His renown for vivid, almost photographic detail, as well as accurate lighting in night scenes and landscapes is reflected in *Spirit of the Night*. Indeed, so magical is his fairy that it brought to life a pixie in *Faerie Magick*.

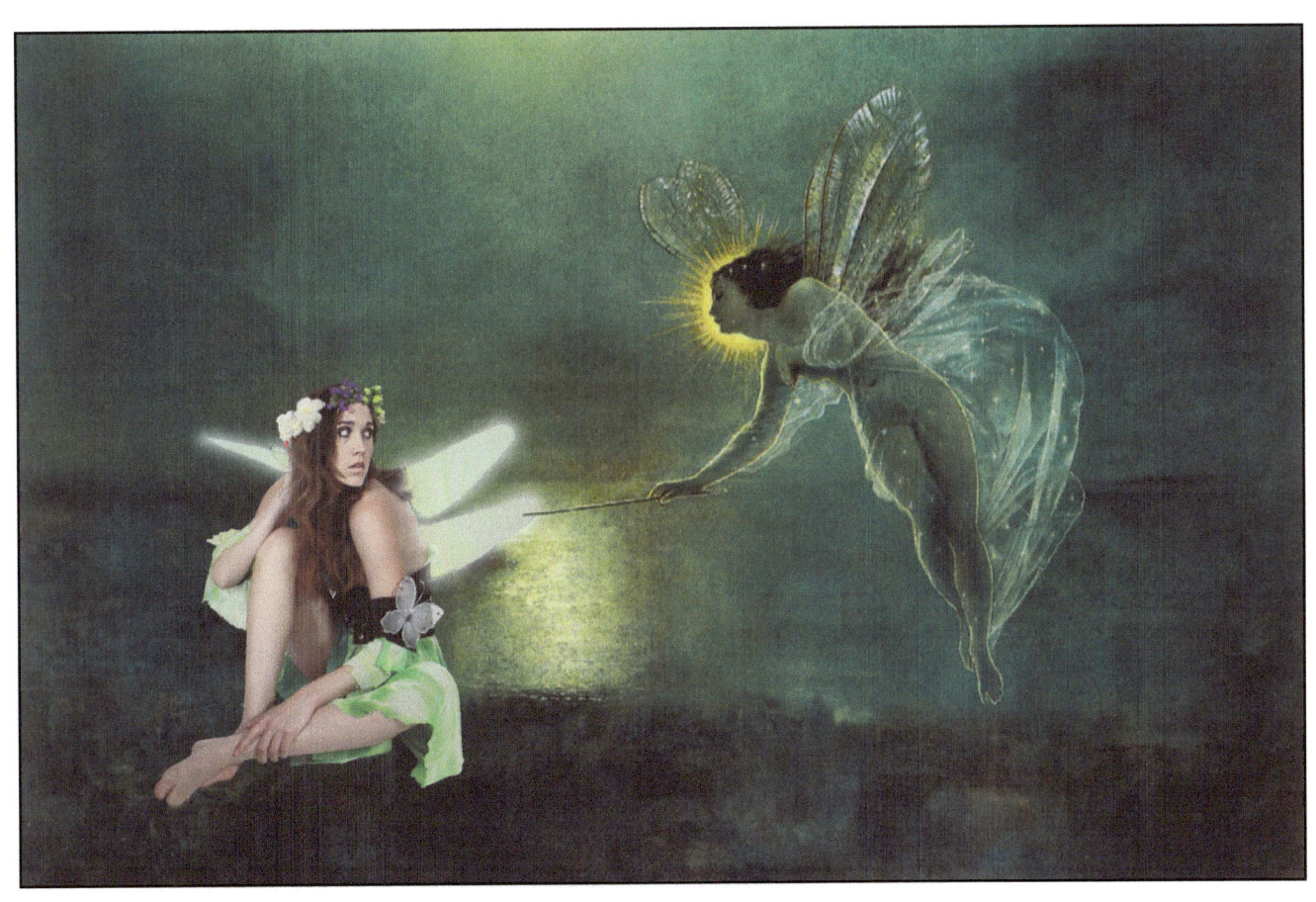

Faerie Magick

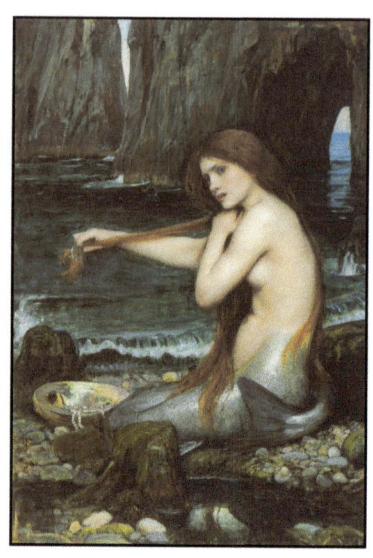

A Mermaid, 1901, John William Waterhouse, 1849-1917

    The son of two painters, John William Waterhouse studied at the Royal Academy of Art. His position as a member of the prestigious Royal Academy was secured by *A Mermaid*.

    Whether mermaids are real or mythological has been argued through the ages. In the first extant mermaid story, dating back to 1000 BC in Assyria, the goddess Atargatis loved a mortal shepherd whom she accidentally killed. Devastated, she leaped into a lake, whereupon she became human above the waist, a fish below.

    In *Mermaid Lagoon*, a twenty-first century mermaid joins Waterhouse's creation, perpetuating their mythology—or challenging it.

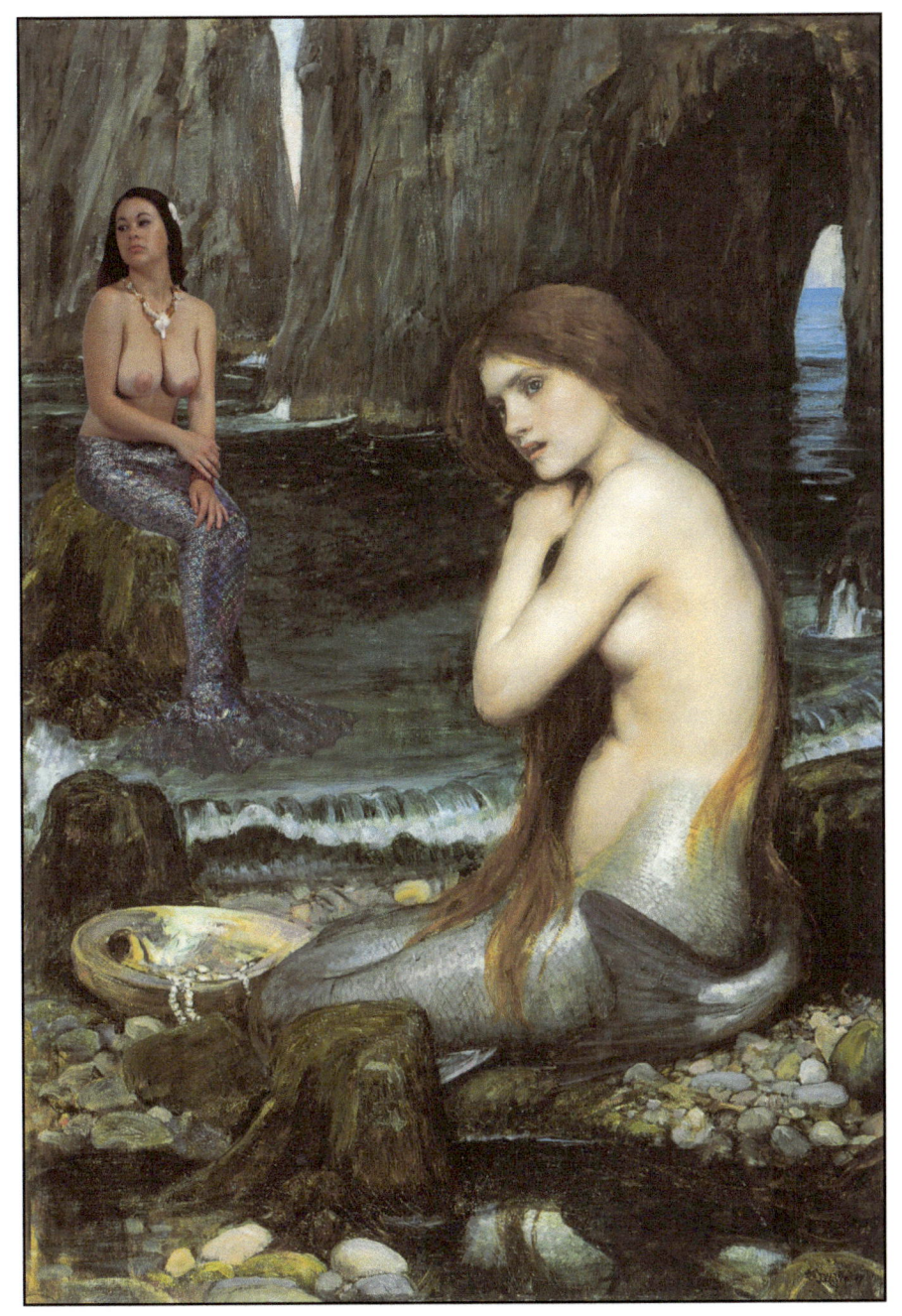

Mermaids' Lagoon

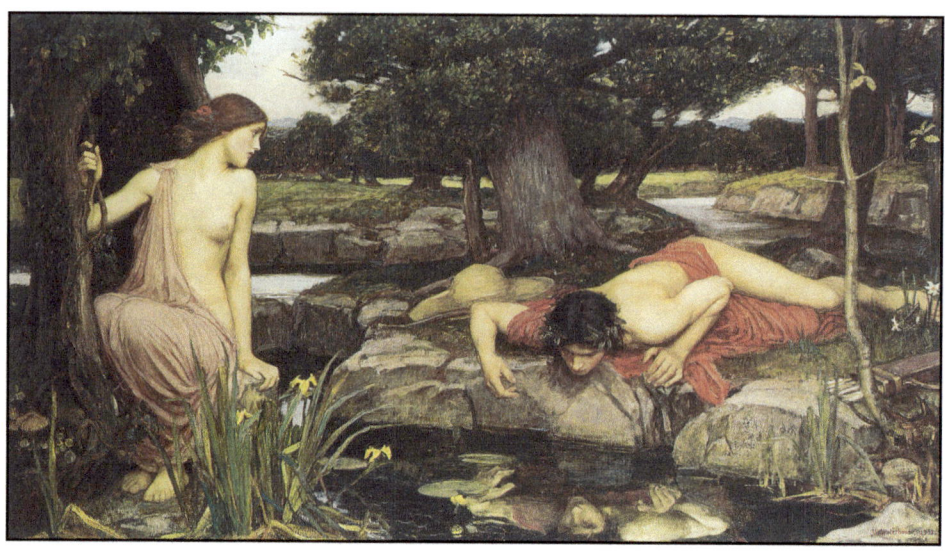

Echo and Narcissus, 1903, John William Waterhouse, 1849-1917

    John William Waterhouse's *Echo and Narcissus* depicts the unrequited lovers in Ovid's Metamorphosis.

    According to *Ovid*, the chatterbox, Echo, fell passionately in love with Narcissus, but he rejected her cruelly. Pining for him, Echo faded until only her voice remained. Then Narcissus, chancing upon his reflection in a pond, fell deeply in love. His attempts to draw the beautiful water spirit out of the pond were repeatedly thwarted, however, and he wasted away until he completely disappeared.

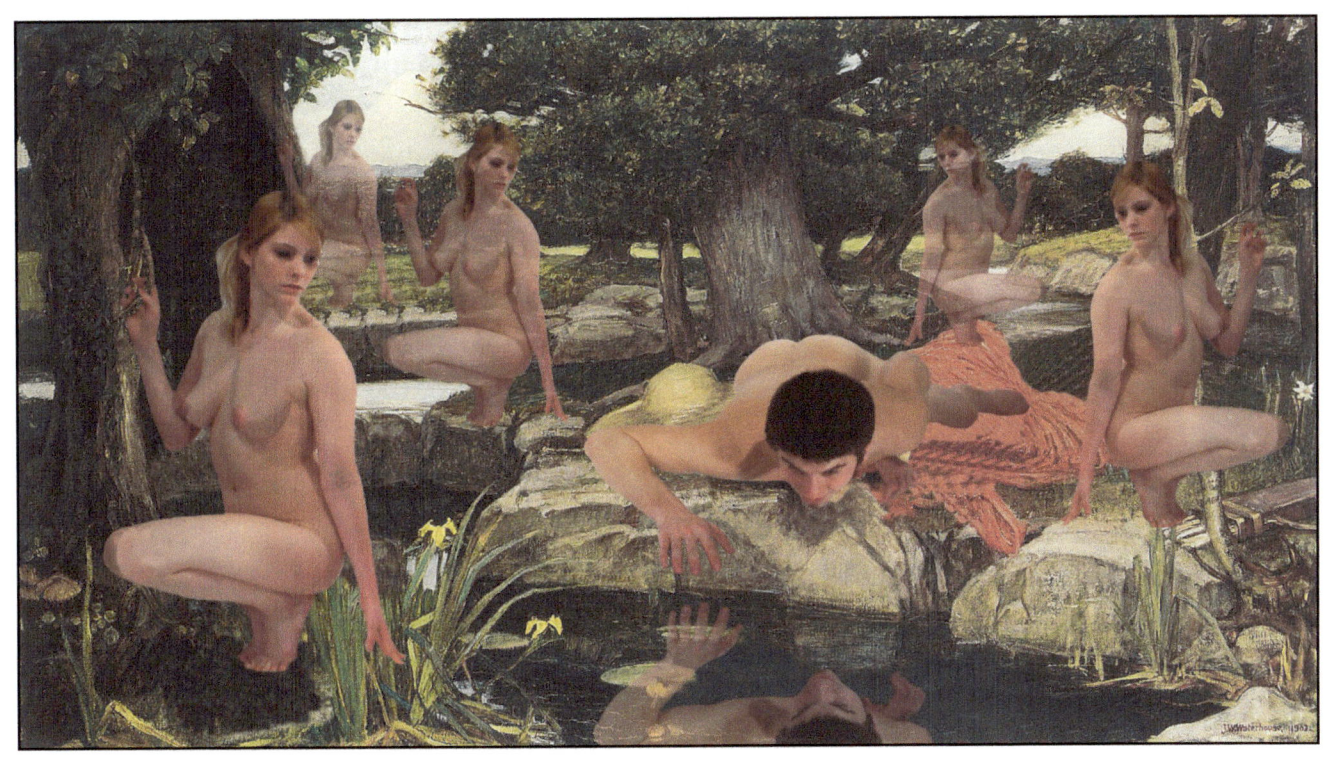

Unrequited

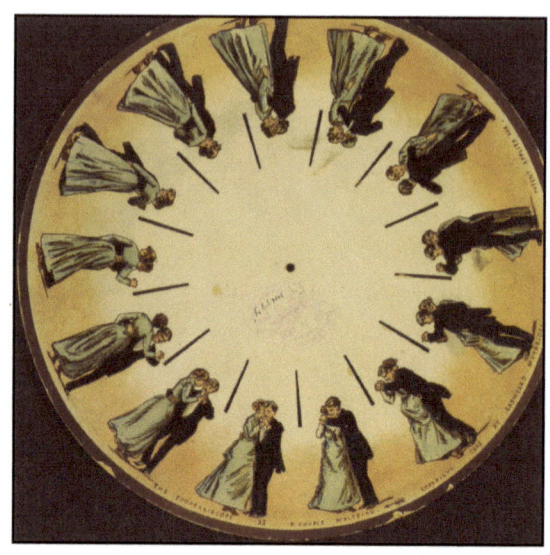

A Couple Waltzing, 1893, Eadweard Muybridge, 1830-1904

    A pioneer in the art and science of photography, Eadweard Muybridge developed the means to capture motion too quick for the eye to see.

    His phenakistoscope discs created the optical illusion of movement, such as a couple waltzing.

    When the disc, *A Seated Figure,* is attached vertically on a handle and spun, the subtle changes in the model's pose become movement.

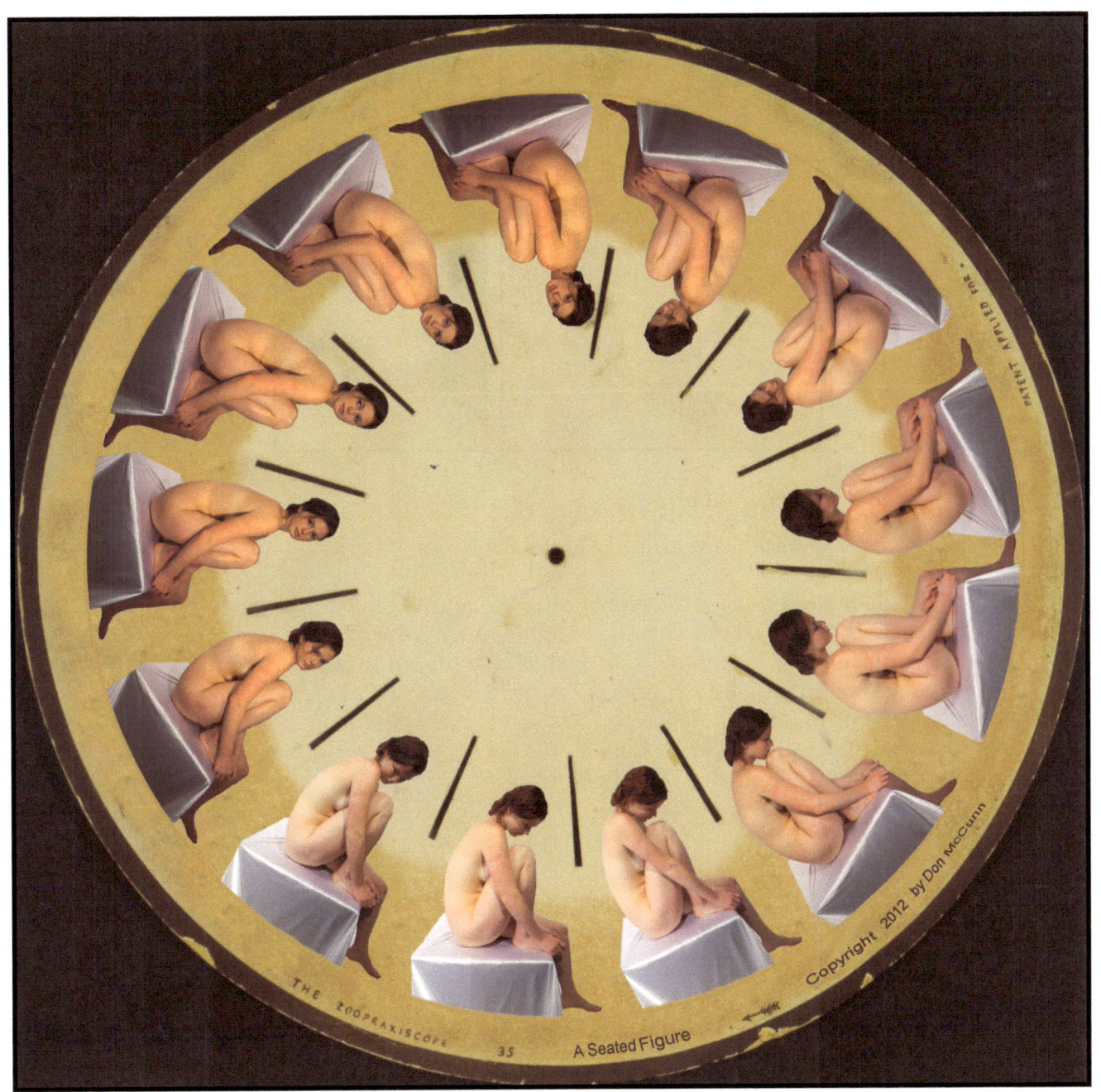

A Seated Figure

21

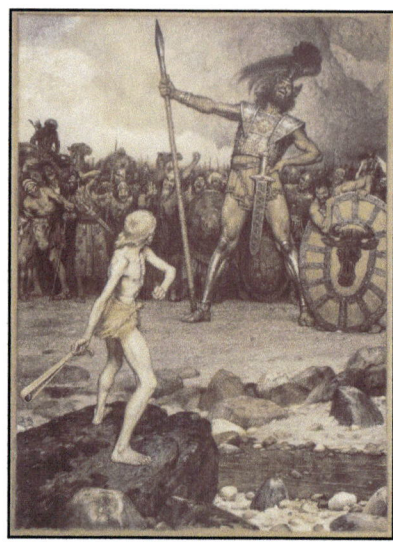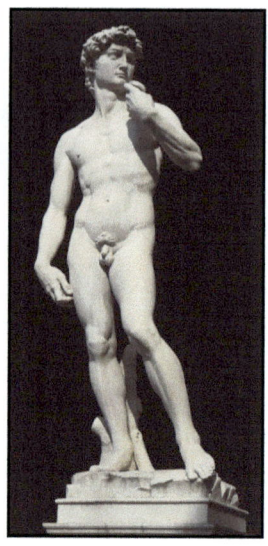

David and Goliath, 1888, Osmar Schindler, 1869-1927
David, 1505-1504, Michelangelo, 1475-1564

The story of little David overcoming the giant Goliath has offered hope
since Biblical times, and although Michelangelo's *David* was originally
commissioned for Florence Cathedral, it was placed in a public square
outside the Palazzo della Signoria, the seat of government, symbolizing
the Florentine Republic's determination to retain its independence despite
threats from more powerful rival states.

In Osmar Schindler's *David and Goliath,* David is swinging the
sling with which he defeated Goliath. But the sling on David's back isn't
obvious when the statue is viewed from the front—even less visible in *The
Last Laugh.*

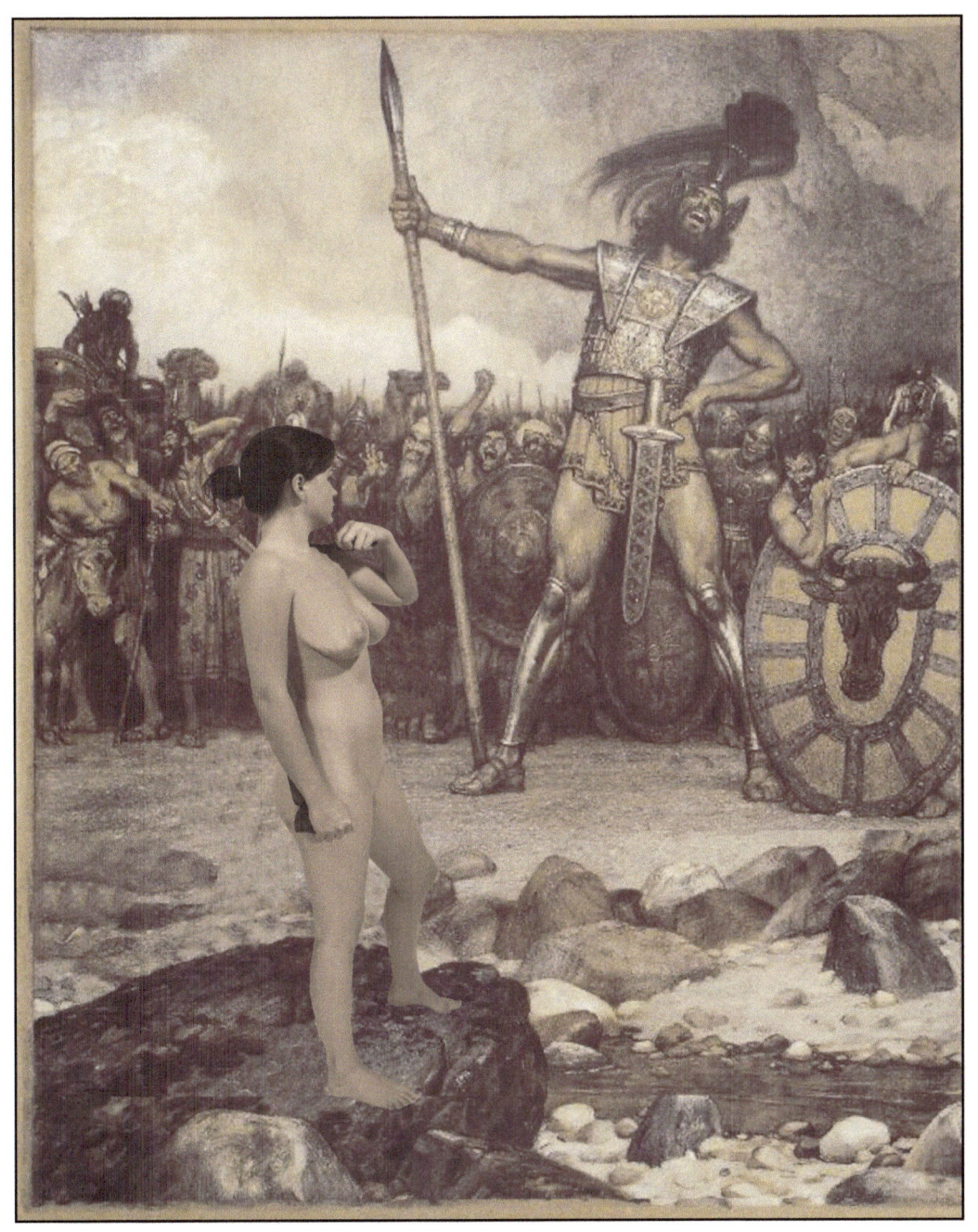

The Last Laugh

23

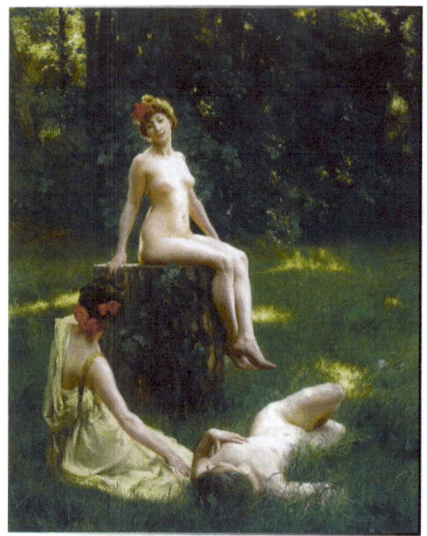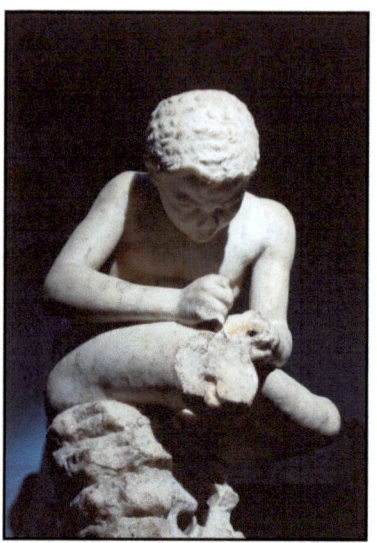

The Glade, 1900, by Julius LeBlanc Stewart, 1855-1919
The Thorn Puller, c.25 to 50 AD

The son of a sugar millionaire, Julius LeBlanc Stewart was an American painter who worked in Paris. Nicknamed "the Parisian from Philadelphia," he enjoyed a lush expatriate life and the luxury of painting whatever he pleased on large-scale canvasses.

The Thorn Puller is a Roman copy of the Greek original—now reincarnated in Stewart's *The Glade*.

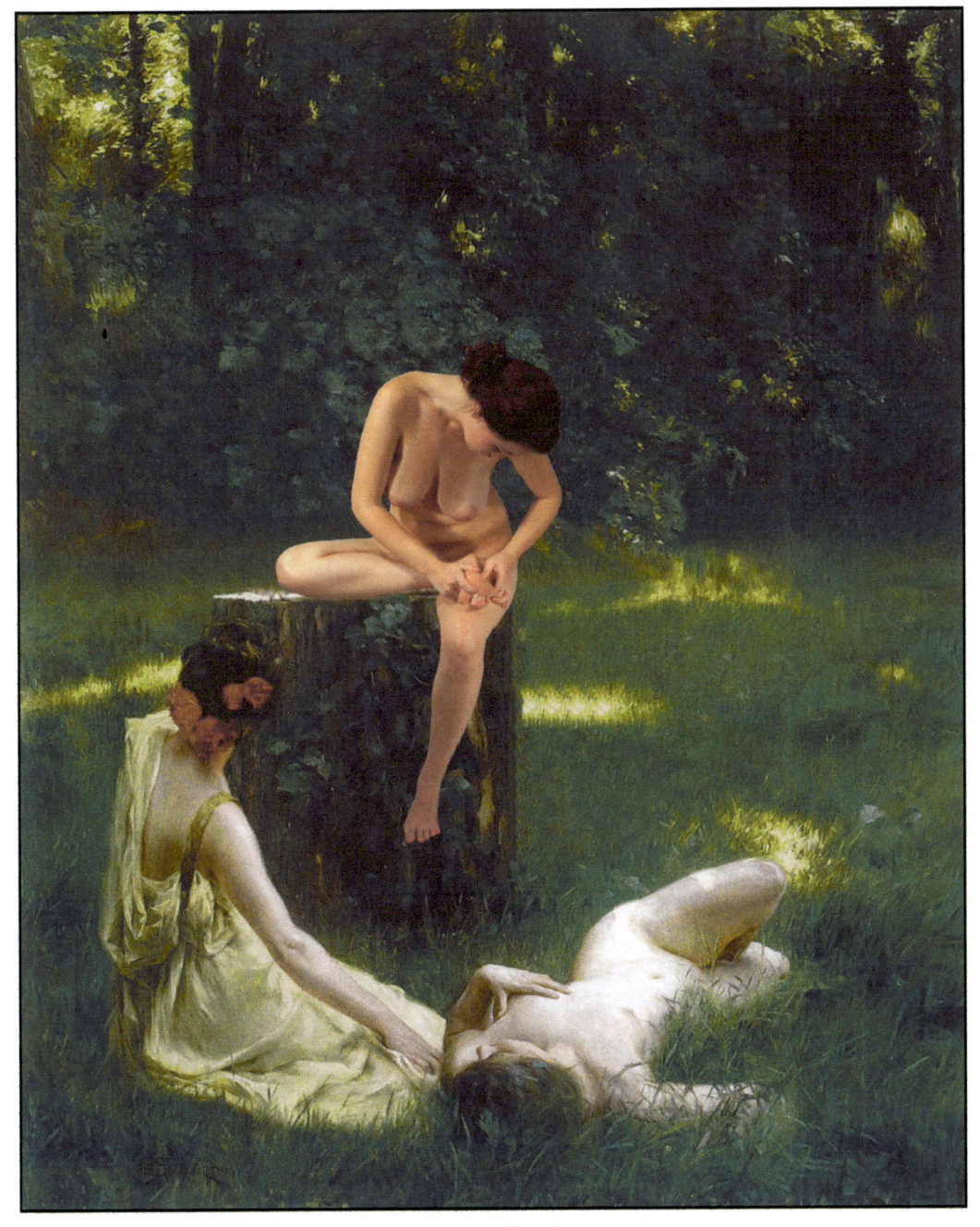

Interlude

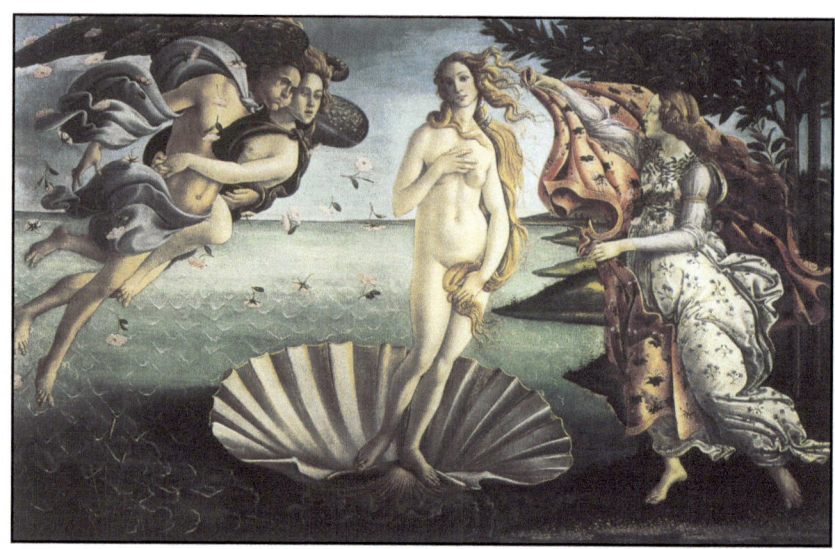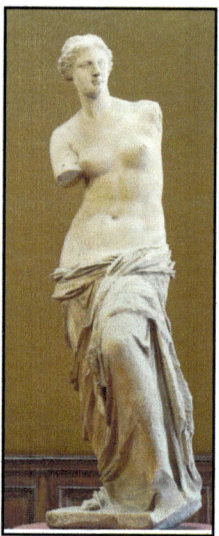

The Birth of Venus, 1486, by Sandro Botticelli, 1445-1510
Venus de Milo, 130 and 100 BC, by Alexandros of Antioch

A treasured masterpiece of the Renaissance, *The Birth of Venus* is among the few mythological works by Sandro Botticelli. His model for Venus—the goddess of love, beauty, and sexuality—was Simonetta, who died young and for whom Botticelli cared so deeply, he expressed the wish to be buried at her feet.

In the myth, Cronus severed his father's genitals and hurled them into the sea. From the foam, Venus arose on a seashell and, aided by Zephyrus, god of the Winds, and the gentle breeze Aura, was carried ashore to be greeted by Horae, goddess of the Seasons.

The pose of Botticelli's Venus has been likened to that of *Venus de Milo*. Since the statue's arms are missing, it's impossible to know precisely how they may have been positioned. *Venus Reborn* is one of several explorations.

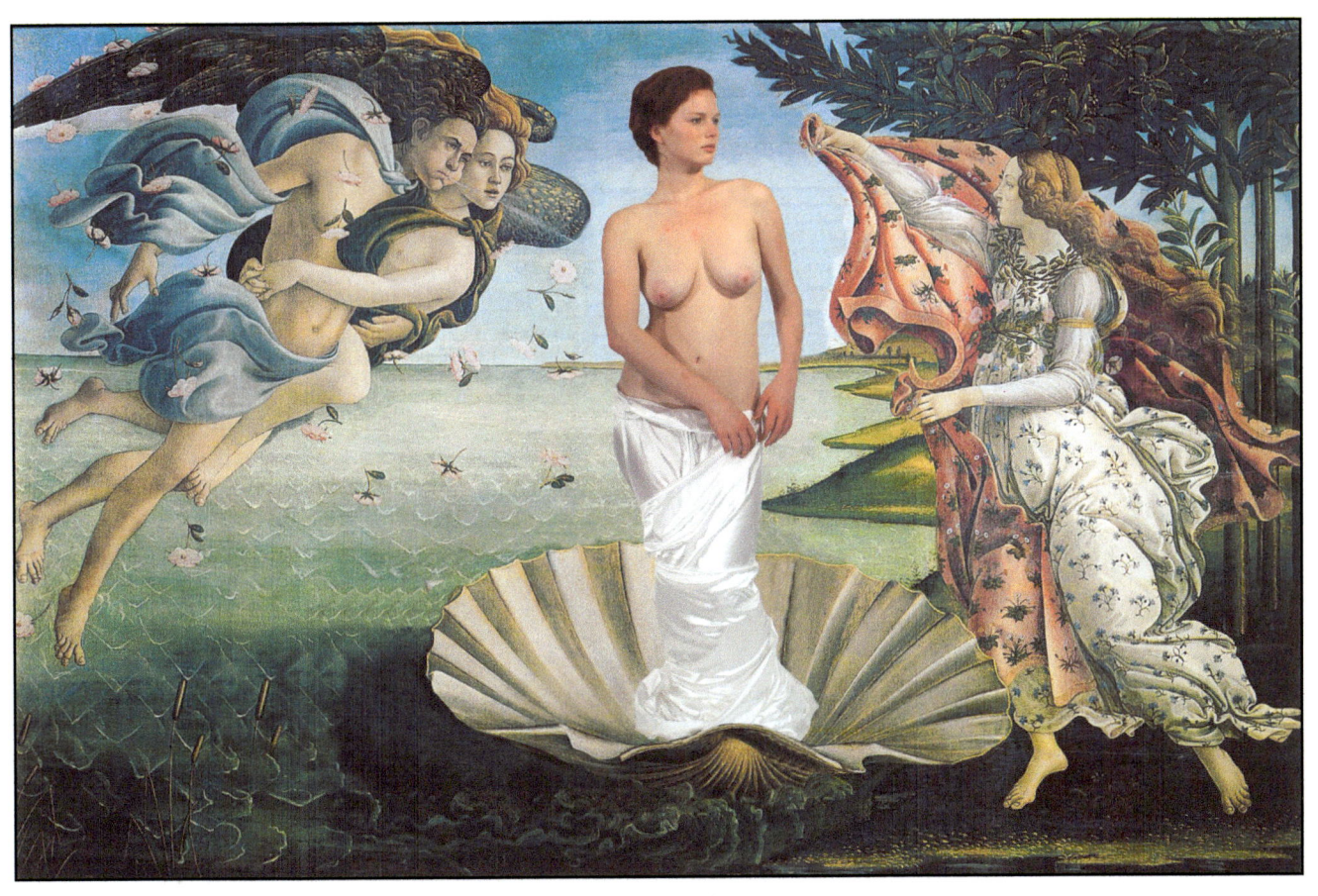

Venus Reborn

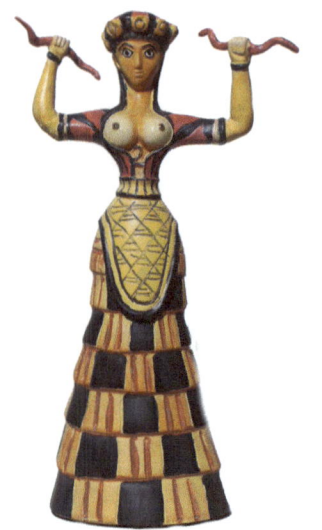 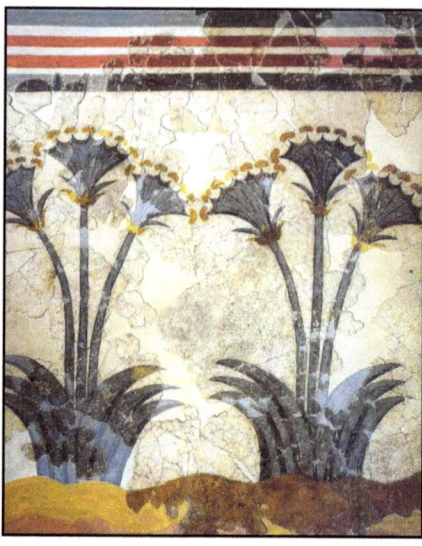

Minoan Snake Goddess, c.1600 BC
Akrotiri Papyrus Fresco, 1600 BC

From the absence of human remains, the inhabitants of Akrotiri apparently received warning of the devastating volcanic eruption that split the island of Thera in two. Prior to its destruction, this important Minoan trade center boasted an elaborate drainage system and an impressive palace as well as buildings faced with masonry and decorated with vivid frescoes. These wall paintings, preserved under thick layers of volcanic ash, have retained their original colors.

The *Minoan Snake Goddess* is considered an iconic representation of this culture in which women held positions of authority in civic and religious life.

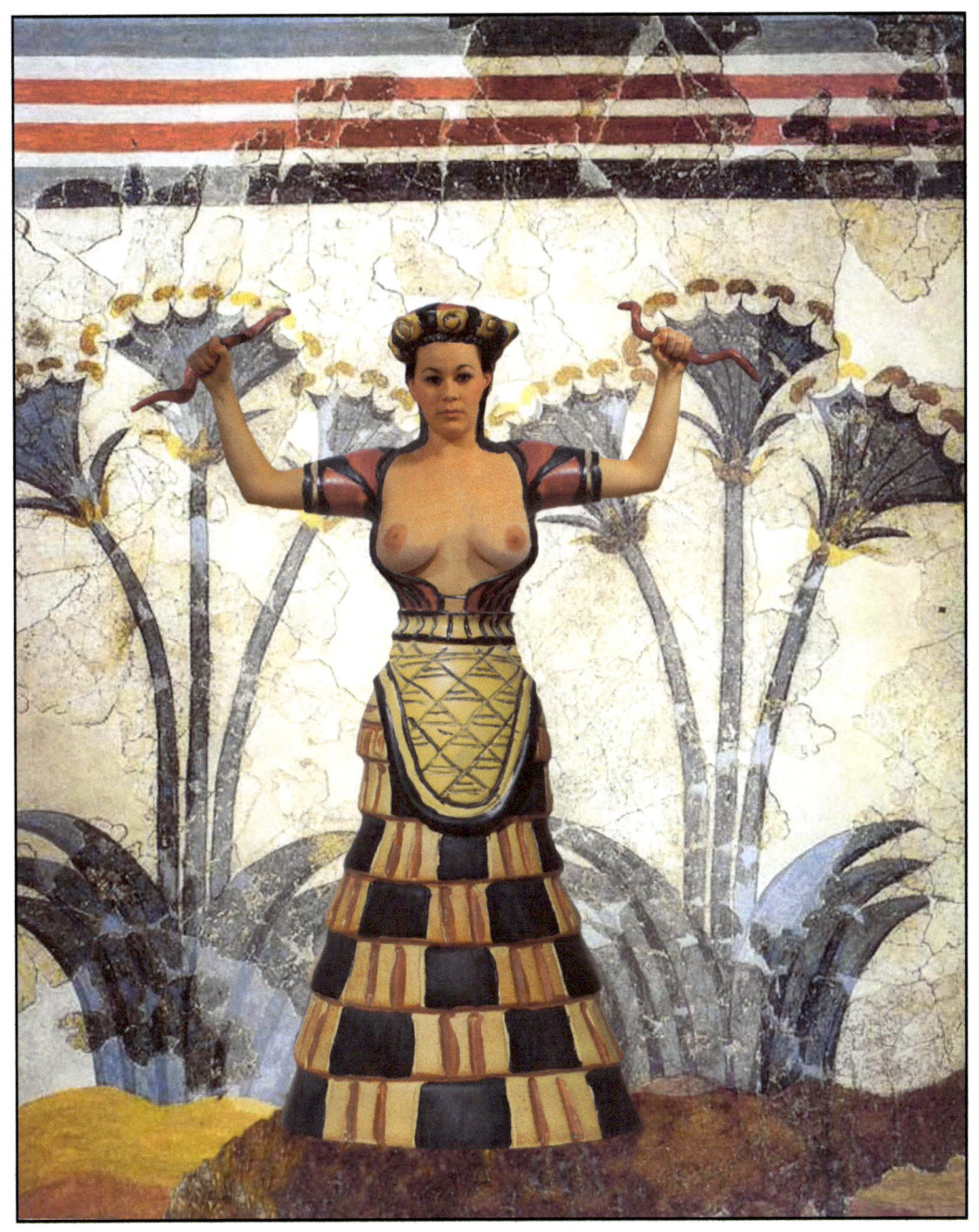

When Women Ruled

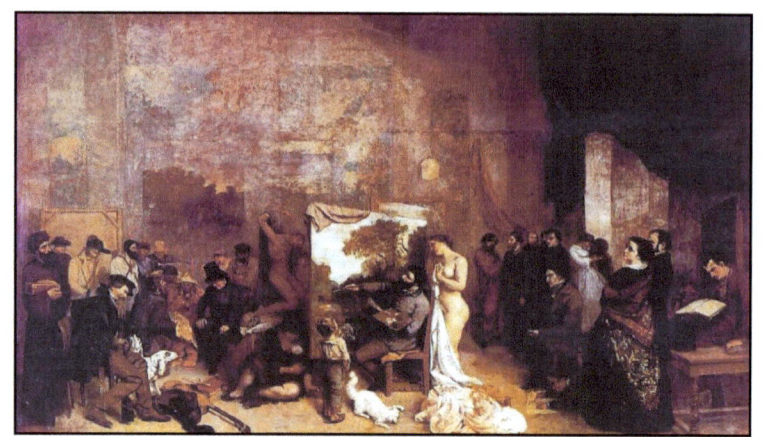 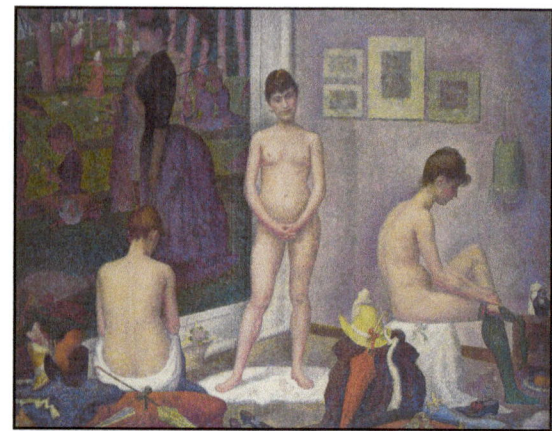

The Painter's Studio: *A real allegory summarizing my seven years of life as an artist*, 1855, Gustave Courbet, 1819-1877
Models, 1888, Georges Seurat, 1859-1891

Gustave Courbet declared, "[W]hen I am dead, let this be said of me: 'He belonged to no school, to no church, to no institution, to no academy, least of all to any regime except the regime of liberty.'" And in *The Painter's Studio*, where he is flanked by friends and admirers on the right, challengers to the left, the opposition is personified by a priest, prostitute, grave digger, and merchant—"the exploited and the exploiters, the people who live off death."

Georges Seurat's pointillist paintings were heavily criticized and rejected by the Paris Salon. Told pointillism could only work with outdoor subjects, he defiantly painted indoor skin tones in *Models*.

Pointillism's tiny juxtaposed dots of multi-colored paint allow a viewer to blend colors optically—rather like the dots used in photographs.

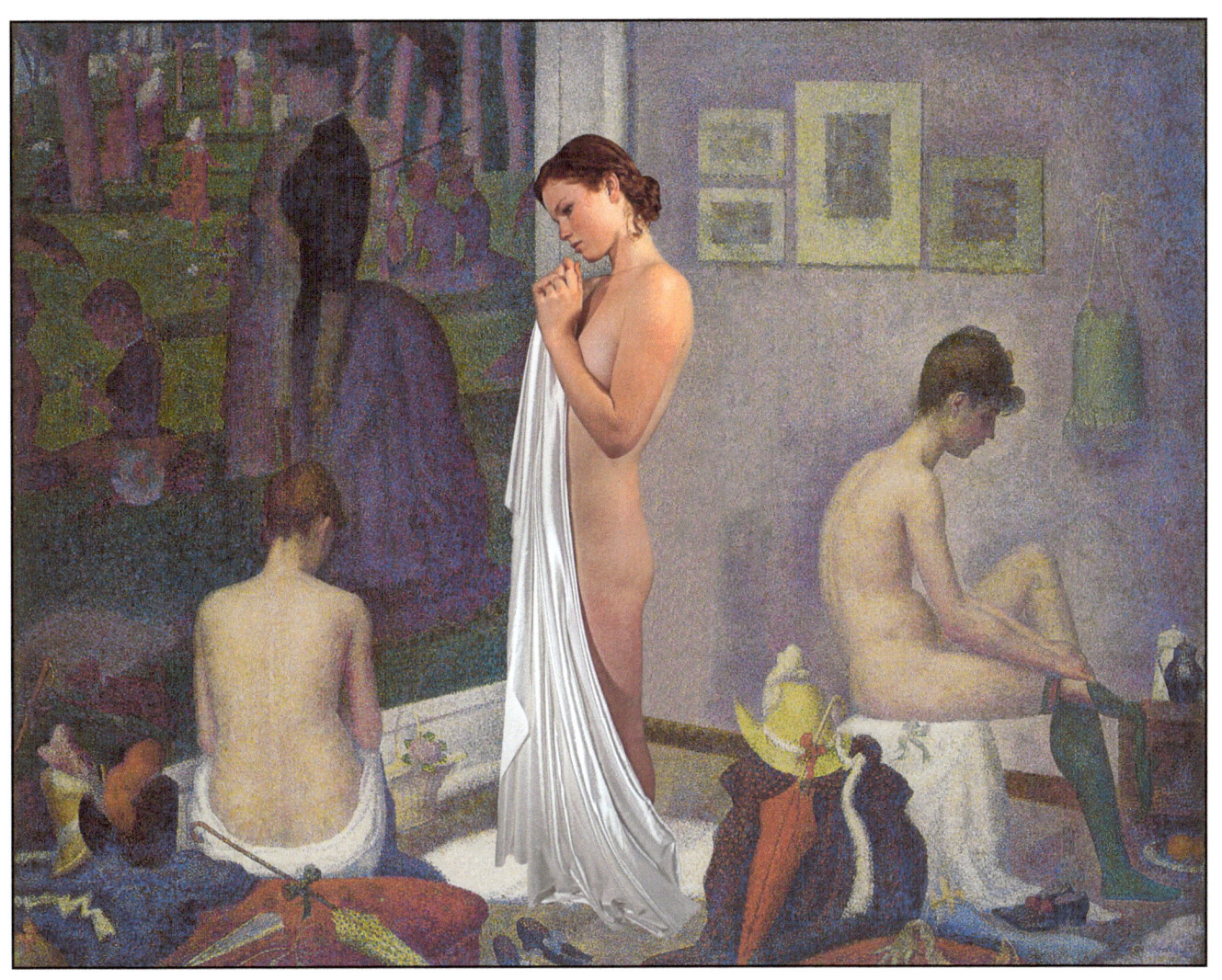

Three Muses

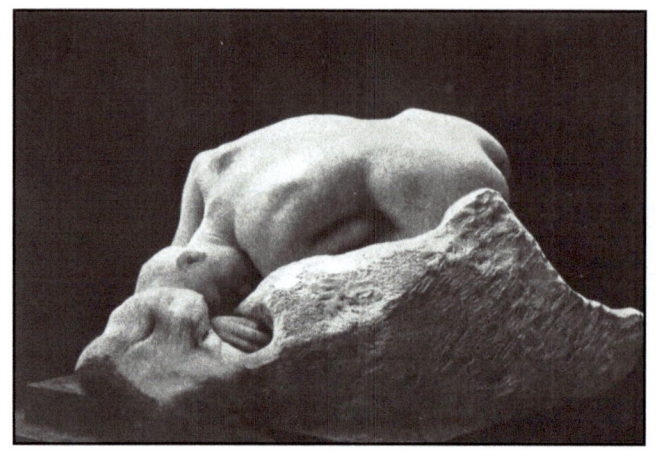 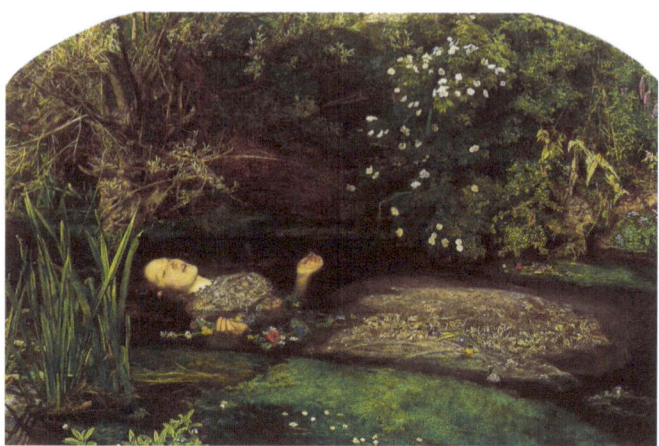

Danaid, 1911, Auguste Rodin, 1840-1917
Ophelia, 1852, John Everett Millais, 1829-1896

In Greek mythology, the fifty daughters of Danaus were compelled to marry the fifty sons of his twin brother. All but one of the Danaids kill their husbands on their wedding night and were condemned to spend eternity attempting the impossible task of carrying water in a sieve.

In Shakespeare's *Hamlet*, Ophelia is encouraged to marry Hamlet. When he tells Ophelia, "Get thee to a nunnery.... I say we will have no more marriages," Ophelia goes mad. By the end of the play, she's fallen into a river and drowned.

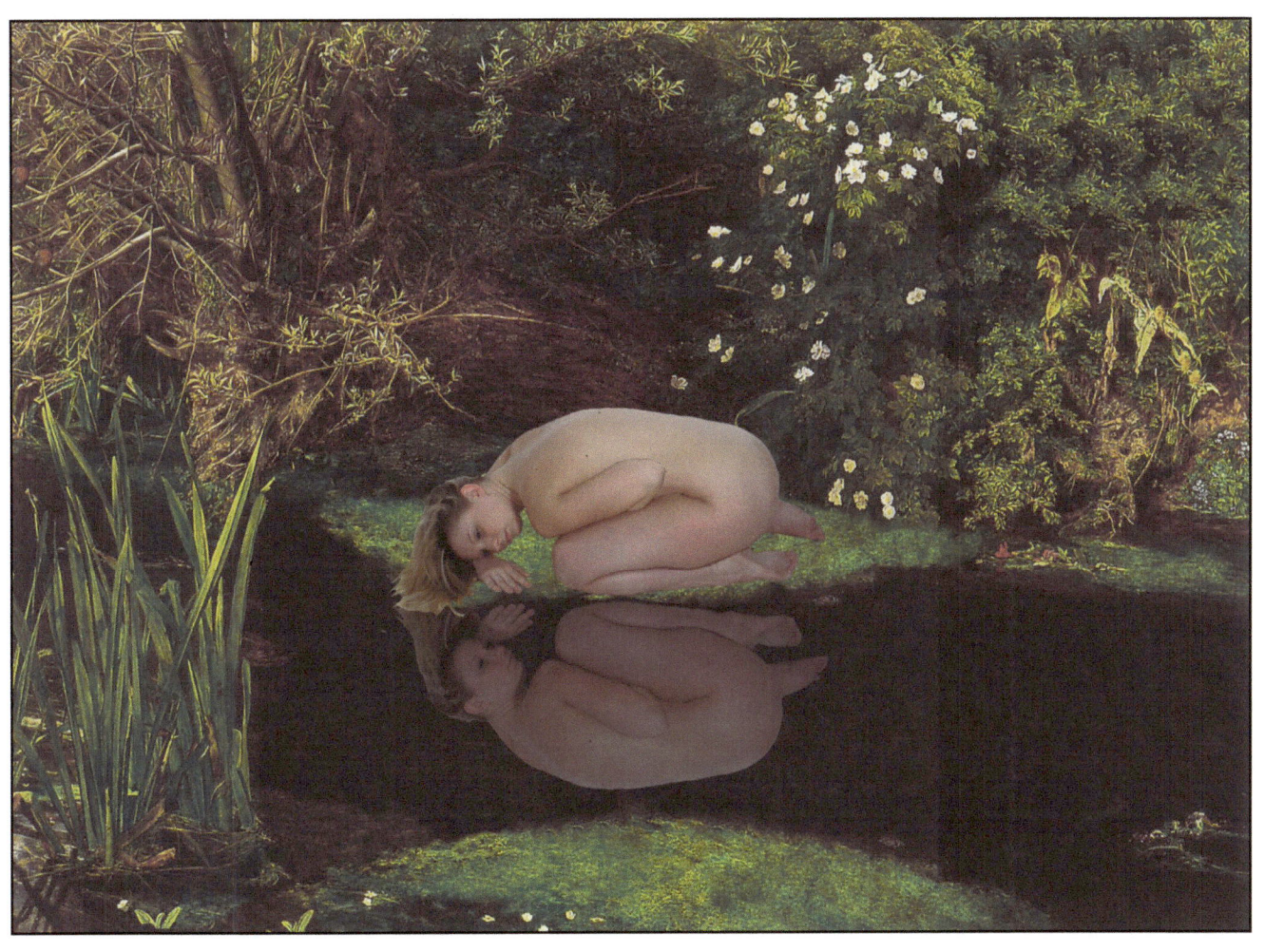

Lady of the Lake

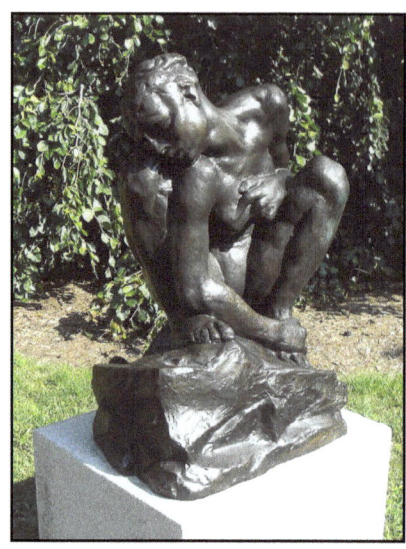 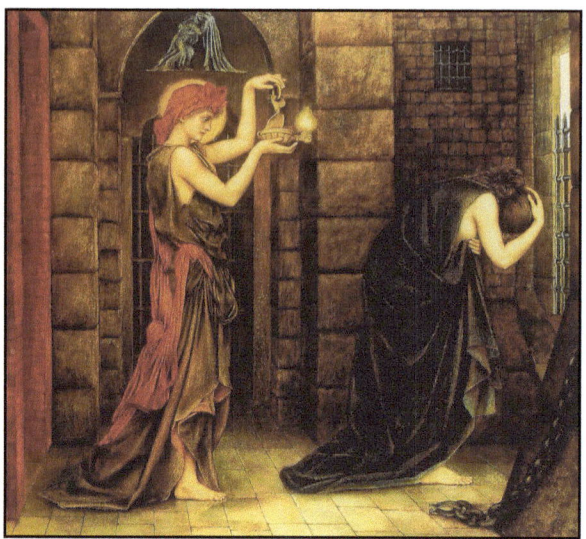

Crouching Woman, 1880-1882, Auguste Rodin, 1840-1917
Hope in the Prison of Despair, 1887,
　　Evelyn de Morgan, 1850-1919

Crouching Woman has been freed from stone for eternity by Rodin's artistry.

Evelyn de Morgan recognized, "Art is eternal, but life is short...I have not a moment to lose." And, mentored by her mother-in-law—a spiritualist and social activist—de Morgan sought new heroines with which to construct original images of Victorian womanhood. Her *Hope in the Prison of Despair* preceded the first English suffragette society by a decade.

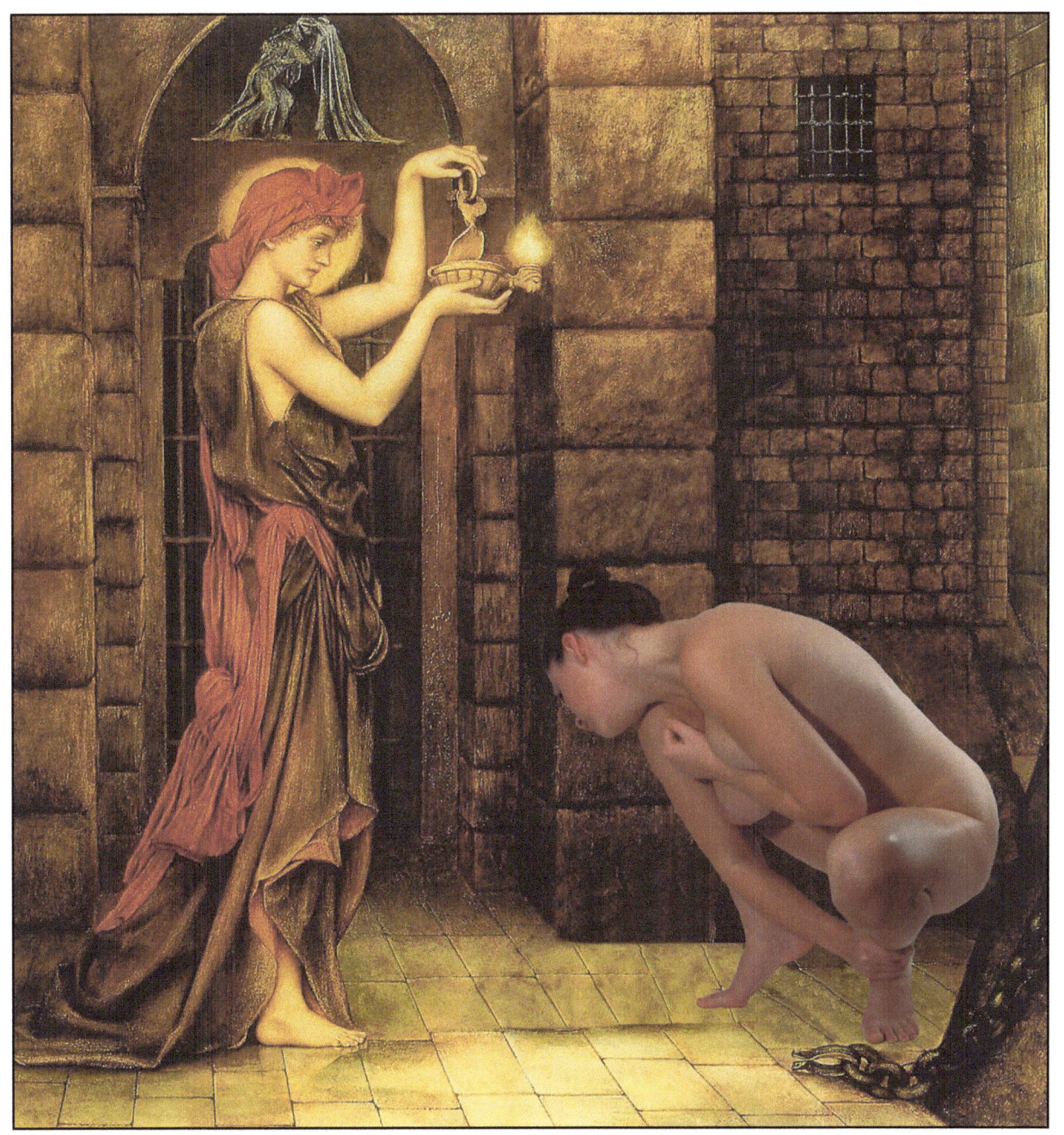

Unchained

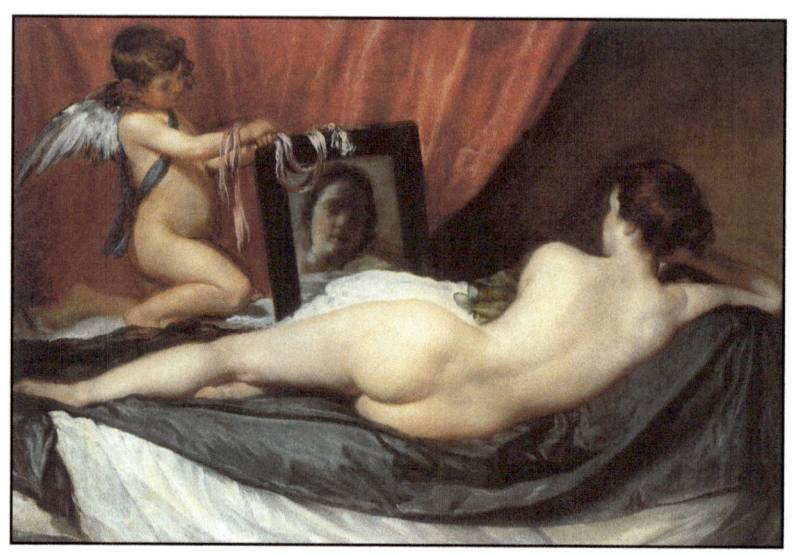

Venus and Cupid, 1649-51, Diego Velázquez, 1599-1660

To avoid censure during the Spanish Inquisition, Diego Velazquez painted *Venus and Cupid* in Italy, then shipped it back to Spain. He took the added precaution of protecting his model's identity by obscuring her reflection.

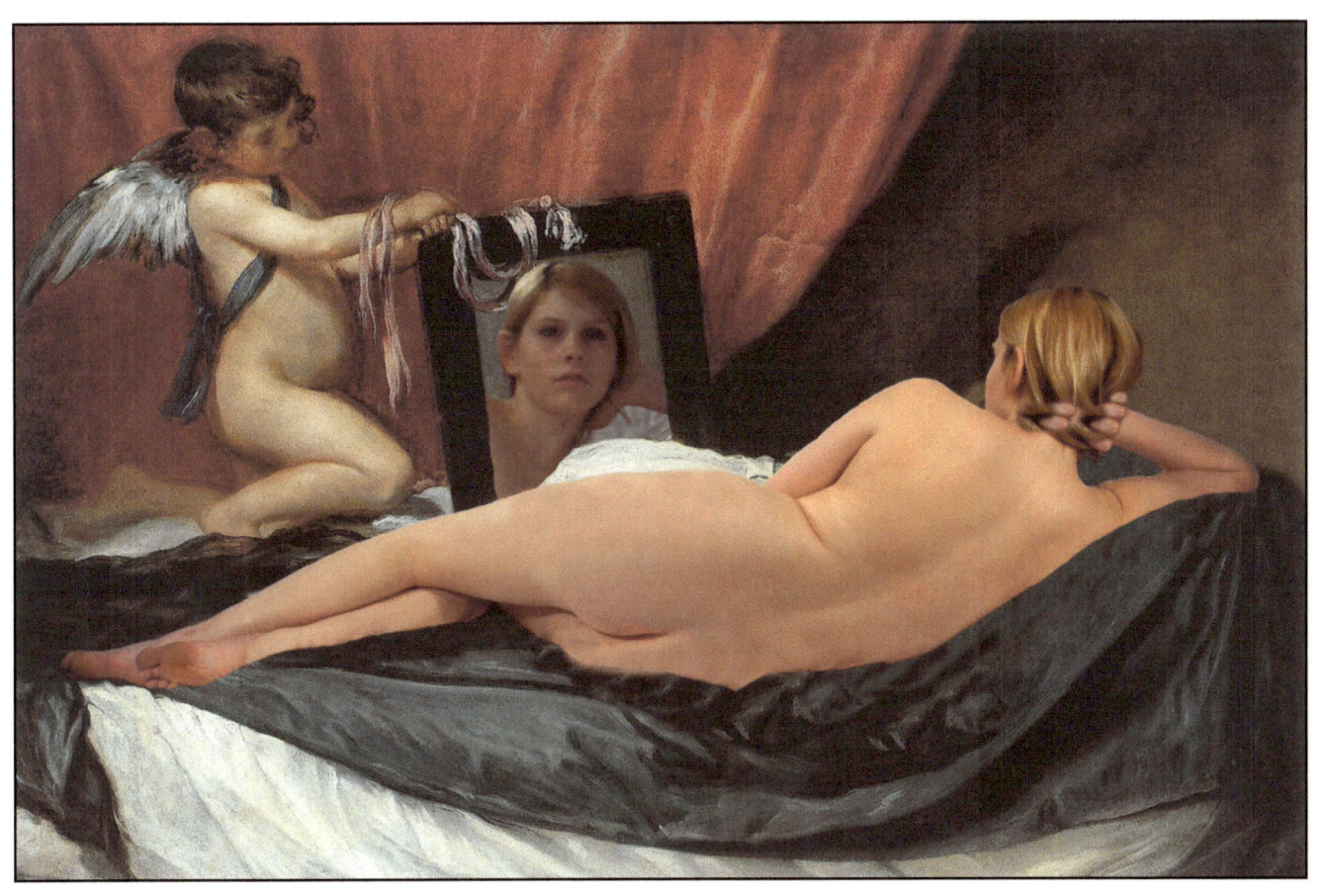

Reflections

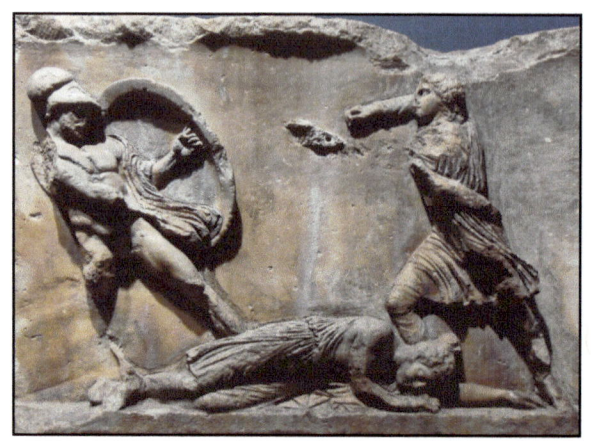 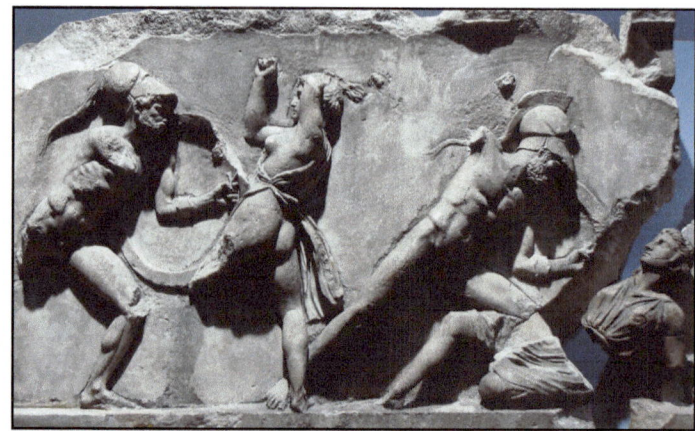

Amazonomachy Frieze, 350 BC,
  Mausoleum at Halikarnassos Scopas

The _Amazonomachy Frieze_ celebrates Heracles' defeat of the Amazon queen Hypolita, and the slaughter of her followers. So it is not surprising that the victors have been depicted as heroic, the vanquished defensive, falling, or dead.

Renowned for their courage, however, the Amazons surely fought bravely even in face of certain defeat.

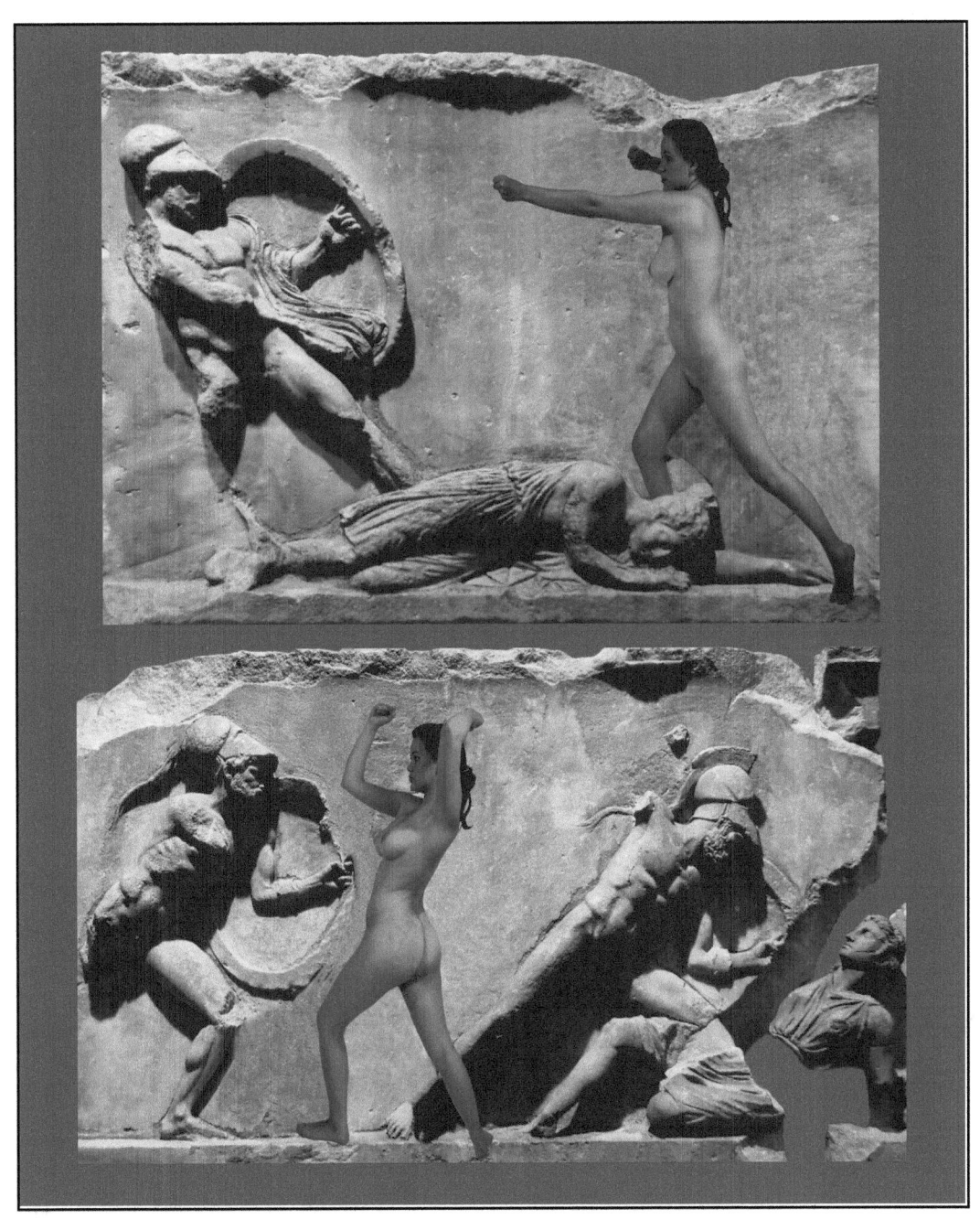

Forlorn Hope

39

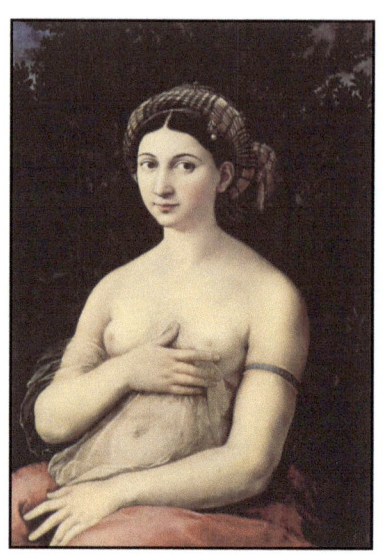

La Fornarina, 1519, Raphael, 1483-1520

Raphael, reluctantly betrothed to a Cardinal's niece, loved his mistress, a lowly baker's daughter, whom he immortalized in *La Fornarina*. A year later, he succumbed to a deadly fever—purportedly after a night of excessive pleasure in the little baker's arms.

Within the year, his betrothed died, too.

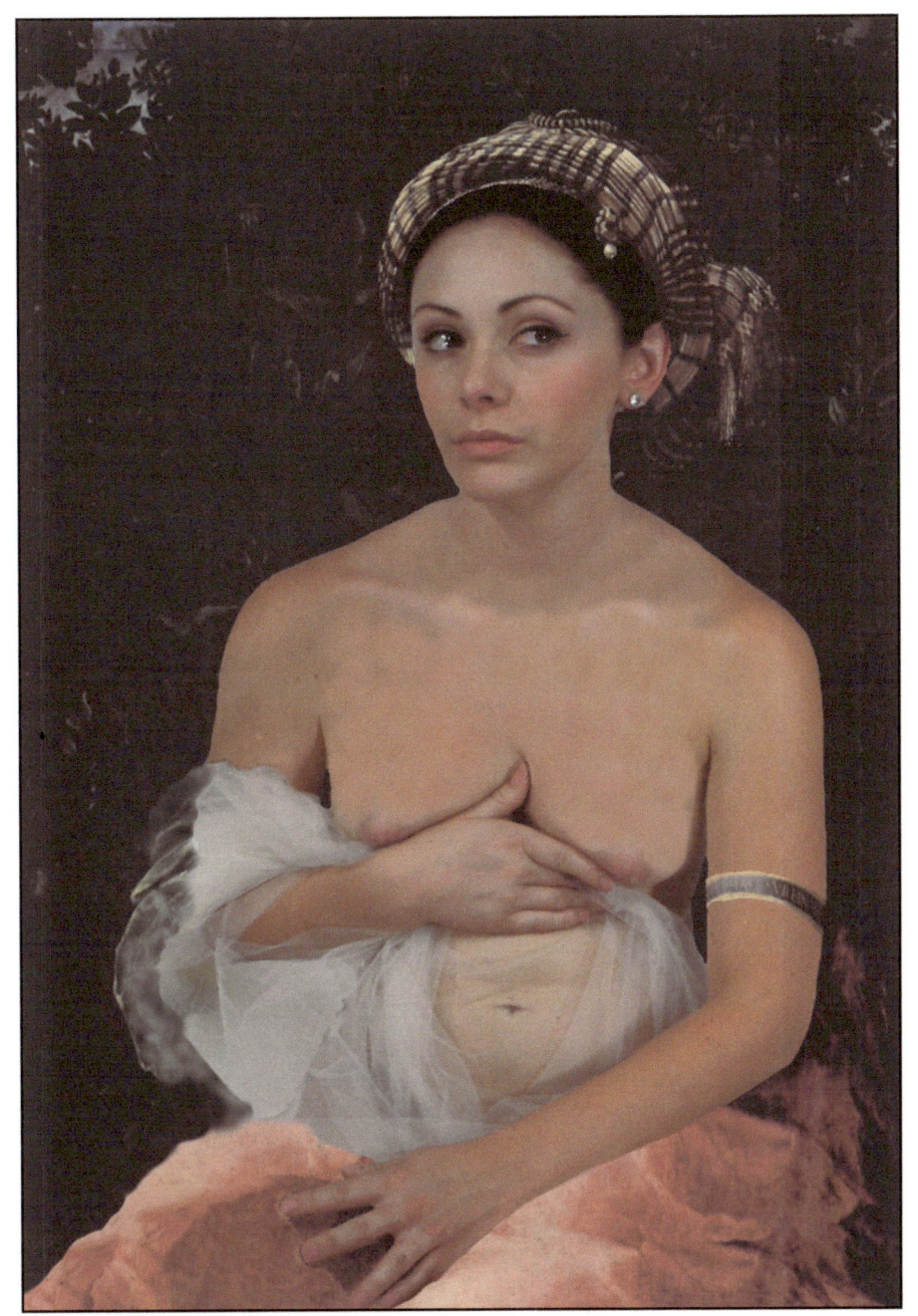

Fatal Attraction

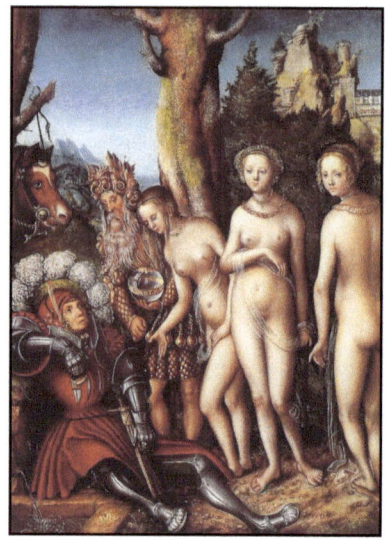 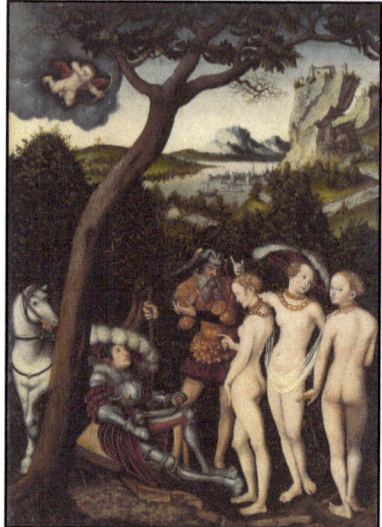 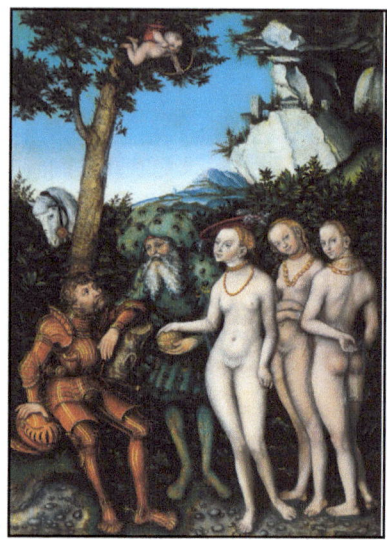

Judgment of Paris, 1512-1514, 1528, & 1530,
Lucas Cranach the Elder, 1472-1553

In *Judgment of Paris*, Lucas Cranach the Elder returned three times to a myth in which all the gods were invited to a wedding—with the exception of Eris, the goddess of discord.

Eris went anyway, and when she was turned away, she angrily cast a golden apple addressed "To the Fairest" into the assembly.

Aphrodite, Hera, and Athena each claimed the apple.

Zeus, asked to mediate, commanded Paris of Troy to decide the winner.

To sway his judgment, each goddess offered him a gift.

Paris couldn't resist Aphrodite's promise to give him the most beautiful woman, Helene, for a wife, and her subsequent abduction led to the Trojan War.

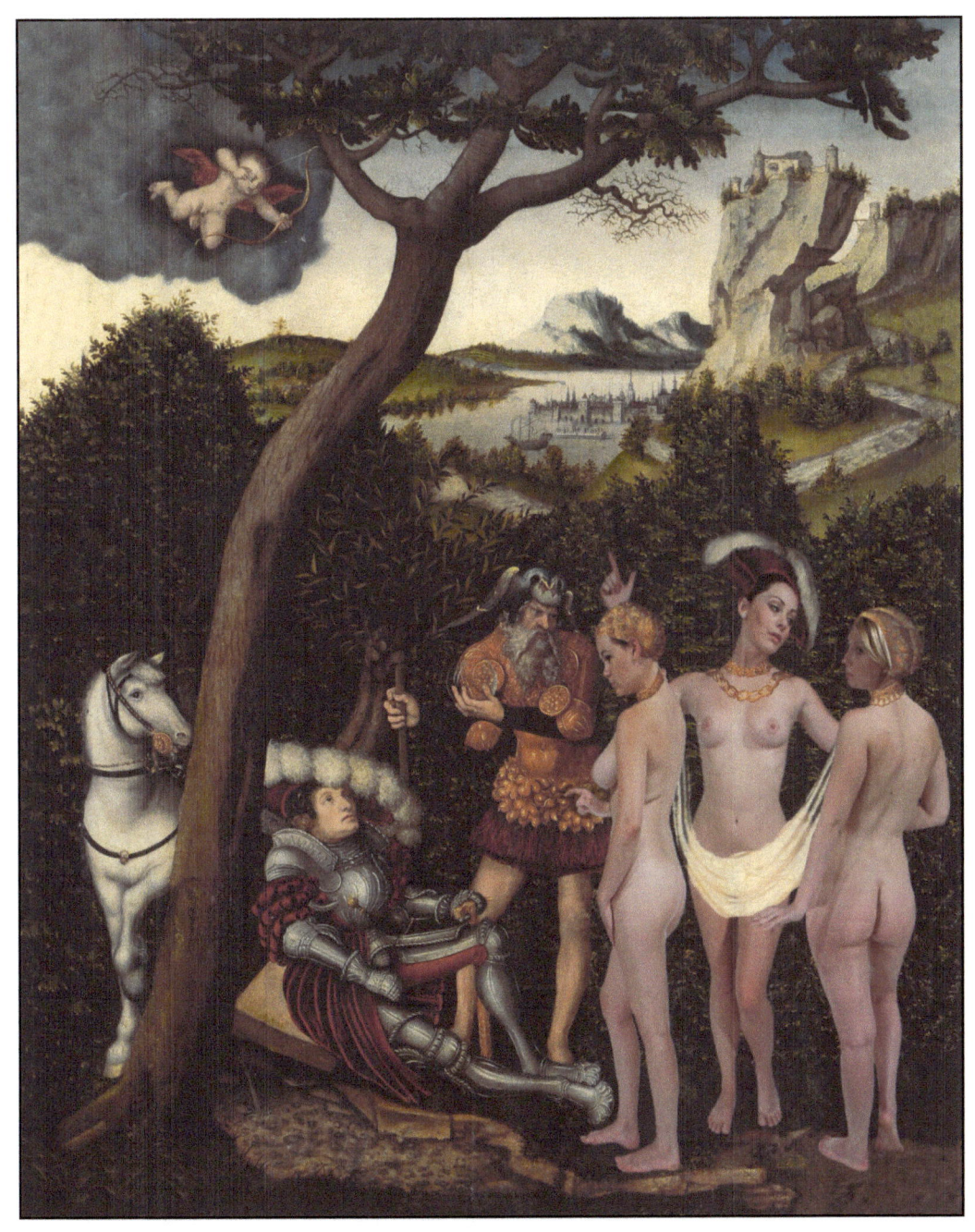

The Beauty Contest 43

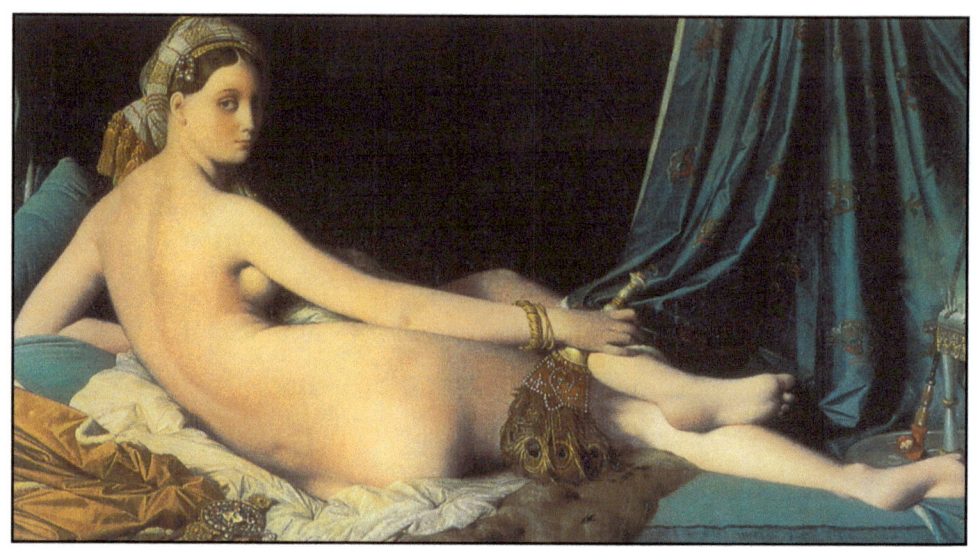

Large Odalisque, 1814,
   Jean-August-Dominique Ingres, 1780-1867

Jean-August-Dominique Ingres suffered frequent denunciations from critics. But many twentieth century artists credited him as a progenitor of their work. Indeed, the artist Willem de Kooning claimed, "None of us would have existed without him."

Certainly Ingres' distortions of the human figure presaged modern art. According to experts, Ingres elongated the figure in *Large Odalisque* by five vertebrae.

Ironically, the Paris Salon charged Ingres with plundering the past because he borrowed freely from the work of earlier artists, adopting whatever historical style he considered the most appropriate to his subject.

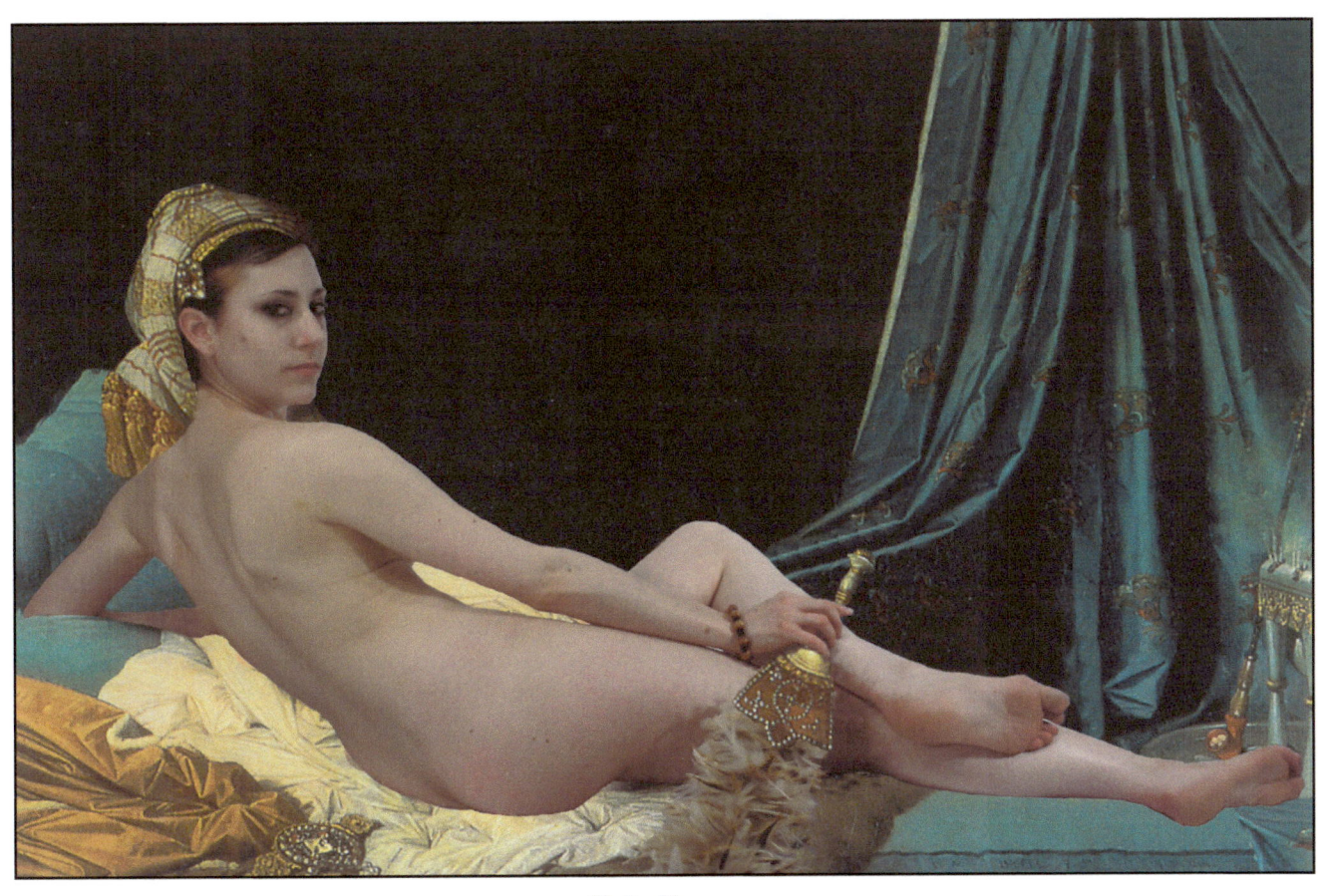

Odalisque

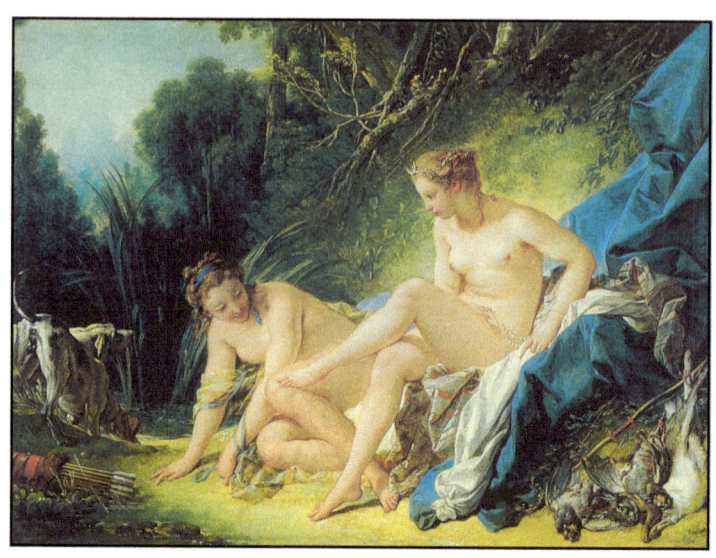

Diana Bathing, 1742, François Boucher, 1703-1770

With the mistress of Louis XV as his patron, François Boucher enjoyed respect and success, becoming the "first painter to the king" in 1765.

Diana Bathing is part of a series for a lavish hunting lodge.

In Roman mythology, Diana was the goddess of the hunt.

Even so, she'd be fair game.

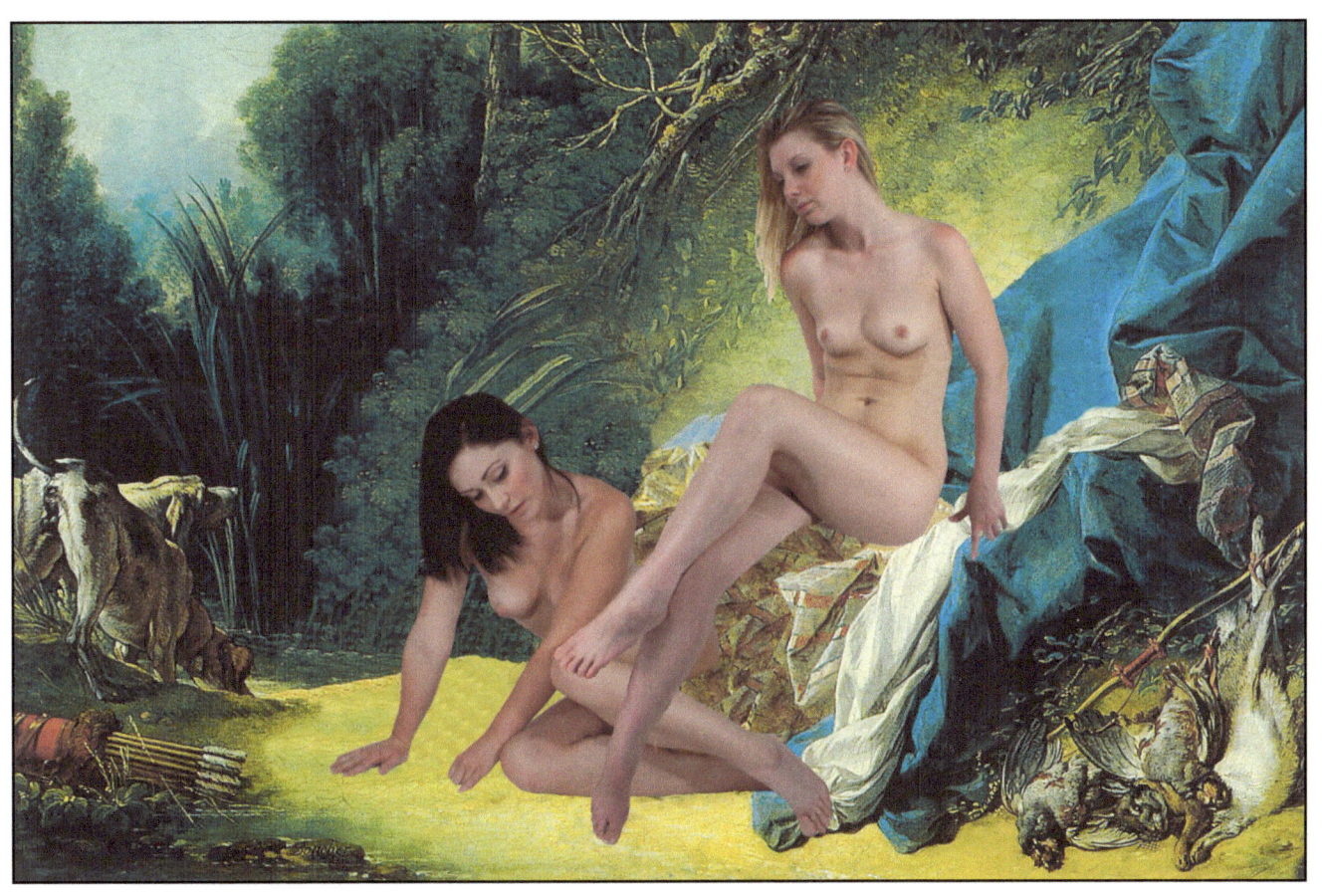

Fair Game

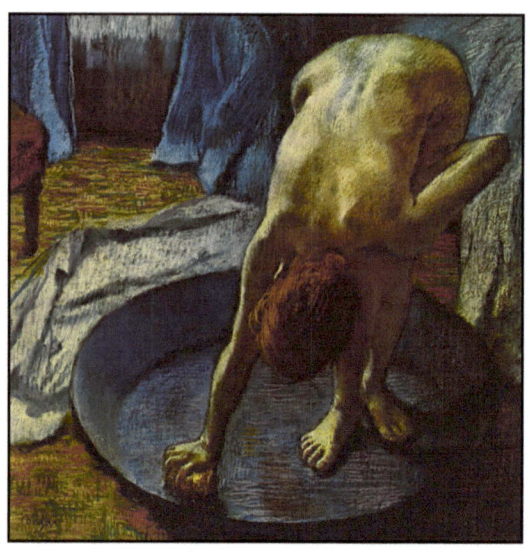

Woman in the Bath, 1886, Edgar Degas, 1834–1917

Edgar Degas' aristocratic family expected him to go into law. While in law school, however, he met the painter Ingres, who told him, "Draw lines, young man, and still more lines, both from life and from memory, and you will become a good artist."

Quitting law school, Degas studied art in Italy and became one of the preeminent artists of the nineteenth century, especially renowned for his portrayals of nudes and performers. Prolific, too! He painted over a thousand portraits of opera and ballet scenes alone.

In his forties, his eyesight began to fail. Undaunted, he switched from painting to pastels and sculpture.

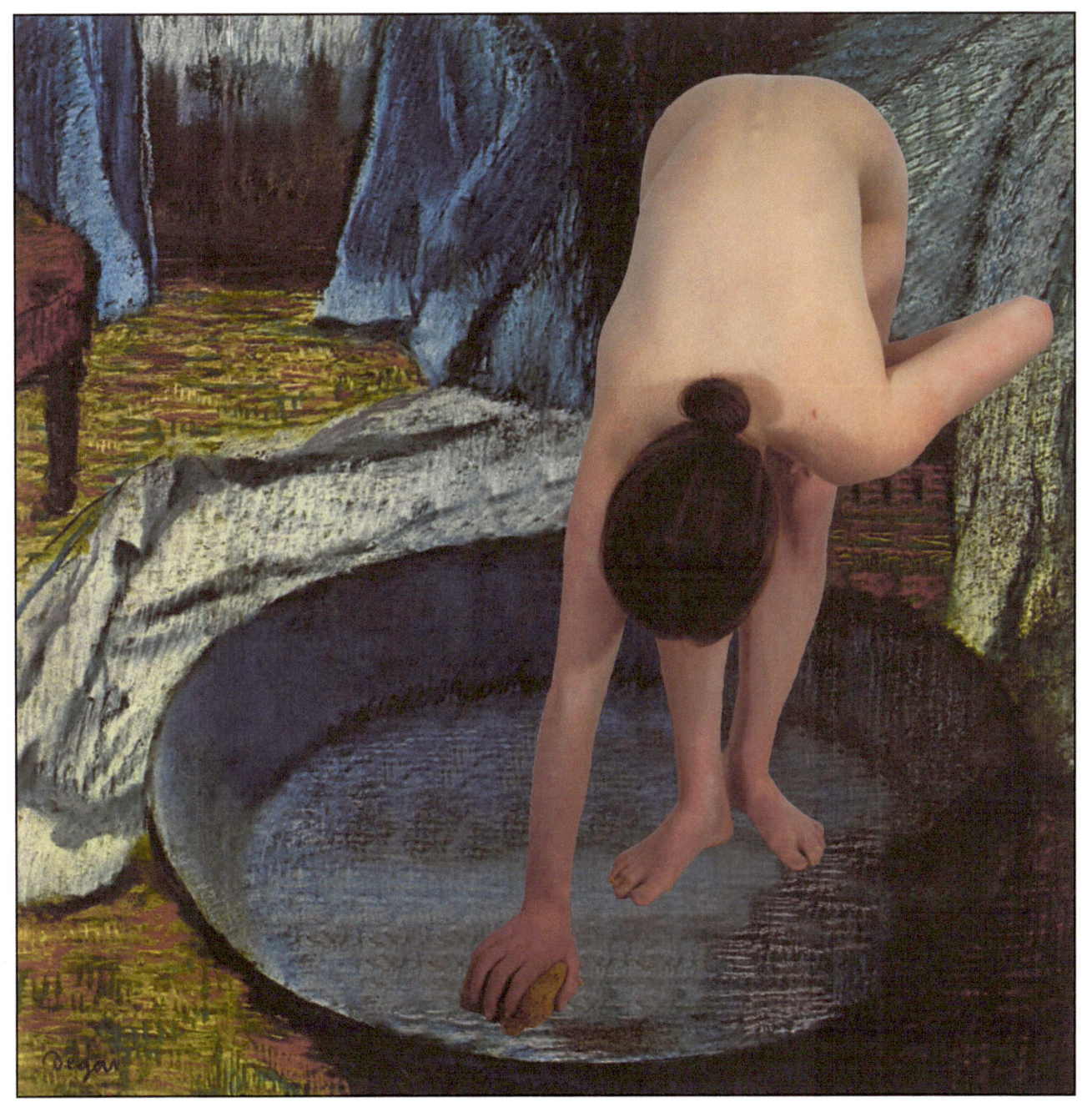

The Bather

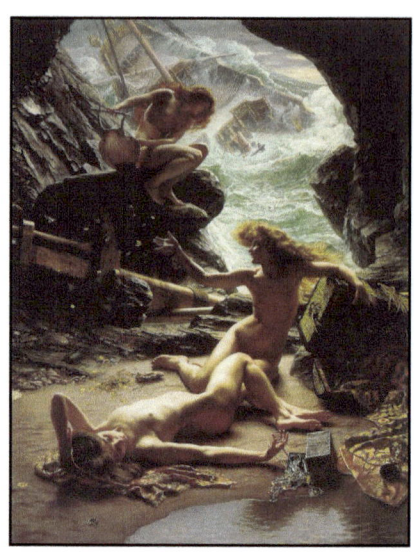

Cave of the Storm Nymphs, 1903, Sir Edward Poynter, 1836-1919

    Sir Edward Poynter, a well respected English painter, became director of the National Gallery and was elected president of the Royal Academy. He did not merely make studies from live models for every figure in his paintings but also did studies of a skeleton in the pose.

    Despite the unpopularity of nudes at the time, he did not shrink from painting them. Nor did he hold back from glorifying sensuality.

    The young women in *Cave of the Storm Nymphs* are clearly enjoying treasures from a destroyed ship.

    Could they be sirens?

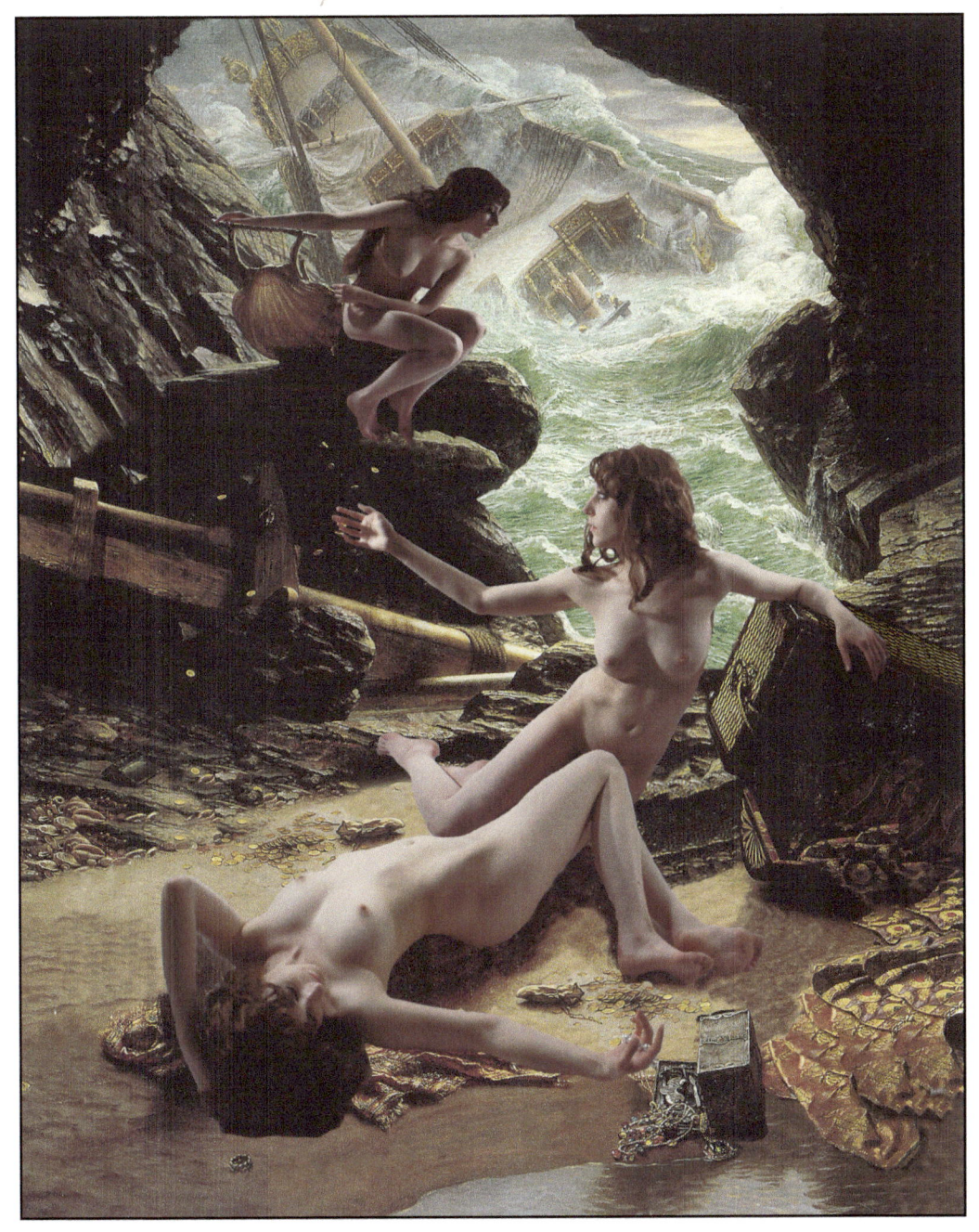

Sirens' Cave

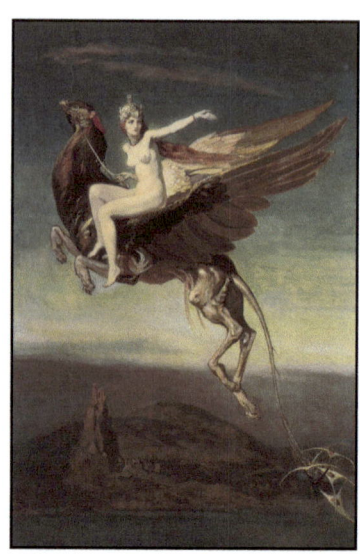

Heptu Bidding Farewell to the City of Obb, 1909,
    John Duncan, 1866-1945

Madman or mystic, the Scottish painter John Duncan heard "faerie music" while he painted.

In *Heptu Bidding Farewell to the City of Obb,* the beast in the painting appears to be a combination of gryphon and cockatrice. Where a gryphon has the body of a lion and the head of an eagle, a cockatrice is born from the egg of a cock incubated by a toad and can turn its enemies into stone merely by looking or breathing on them.

Altogether a *Flight Fantastic!*

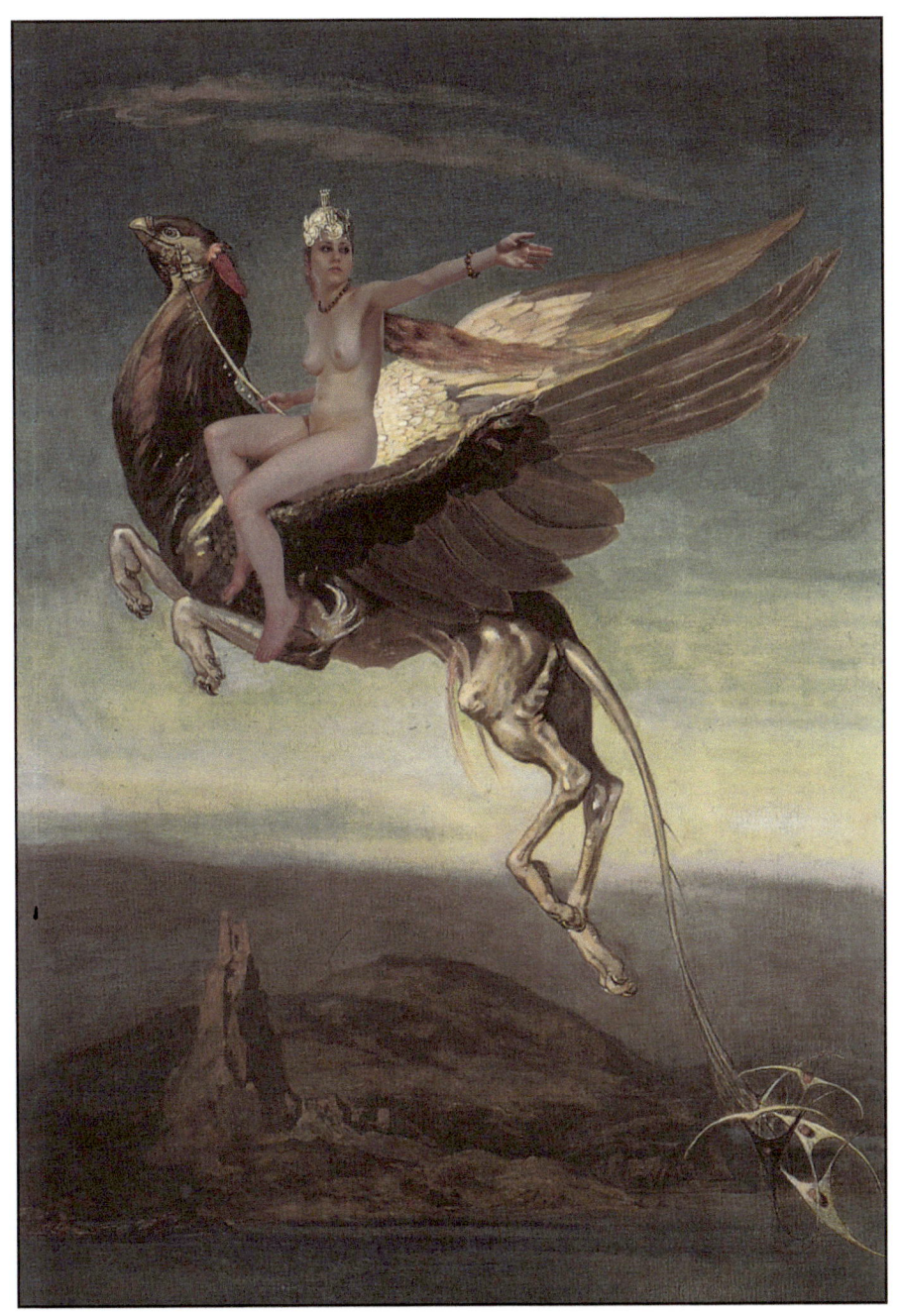

Flight Fantastic

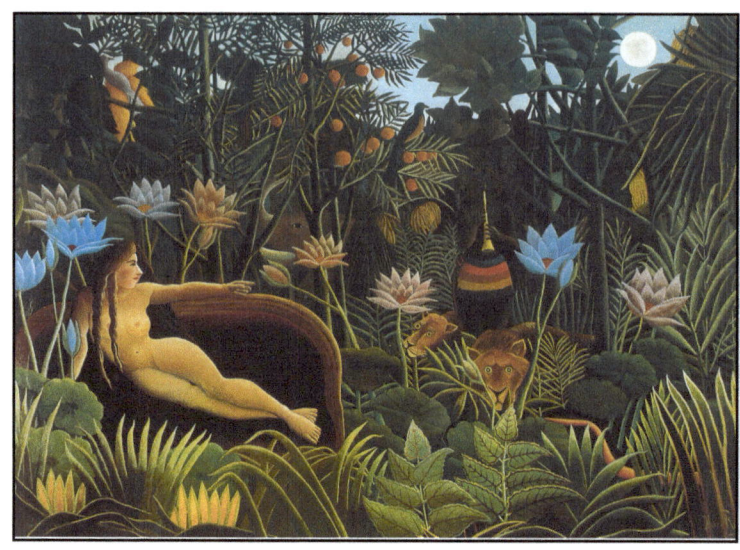

The Dream, 1910, Henri Rousseau, 1844-1910

A toll collector in Paris, Henri Rousseau did not start painting seriously until his early forties.

Critics condemned his work as childish. Stumbling upon one of Rousseau's paintings being sold as canvas to be painted over, however, Pablo Picasso recognized the self-taught artist's genius.

Rousseau's inspiration came from books and the botanical gardens in Paris. He said, "When I go into the glass houses and I see the strange plants of exotic lands, it seems to me that I enter into a dream."

The Dream was his final painting.

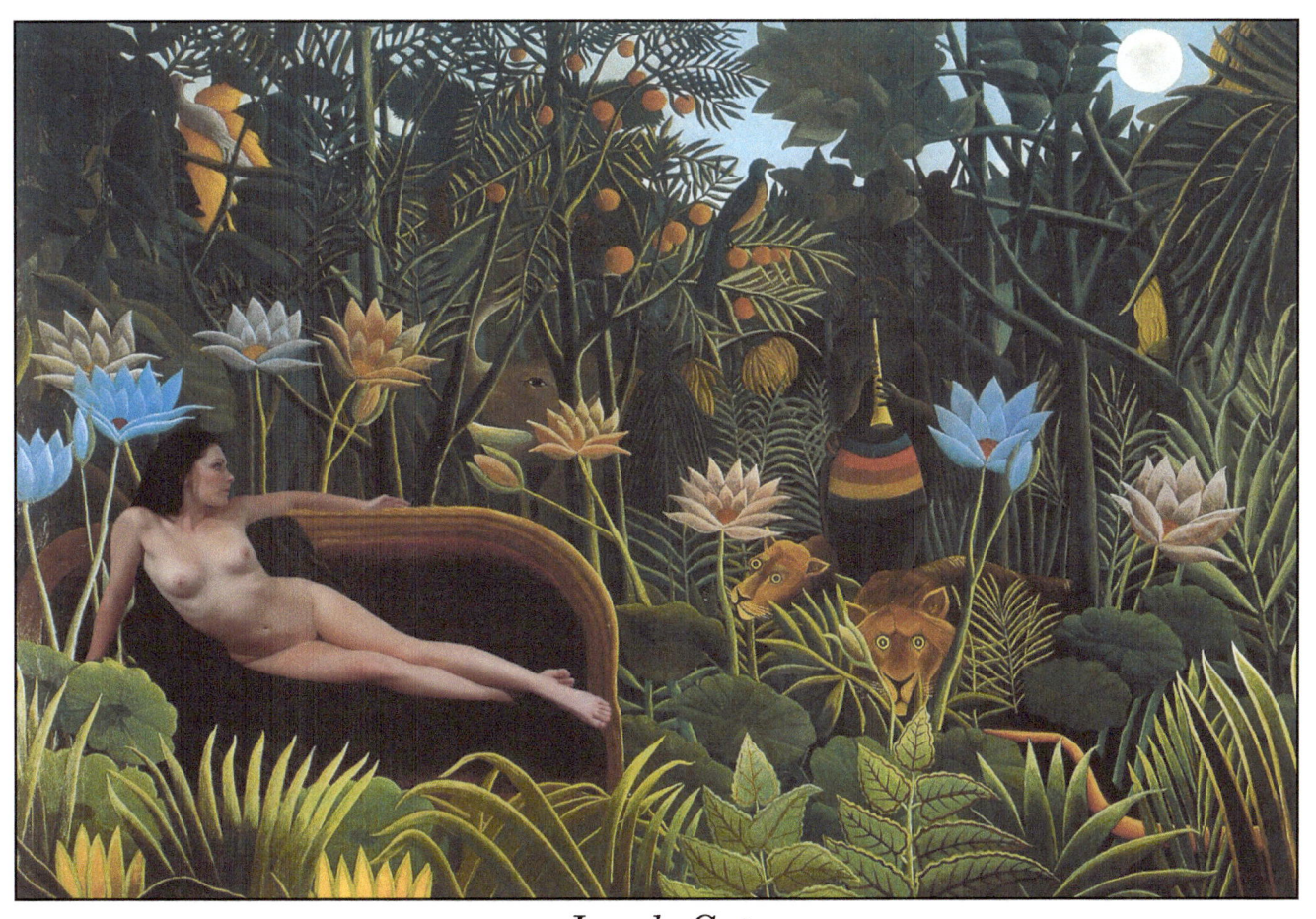

Jungle Cats

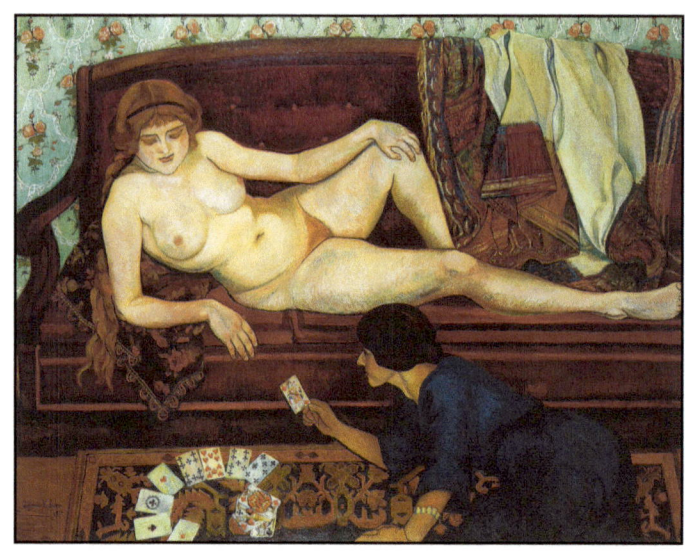

The Future Unveiled, 1912, Suzanne Valadon, 1865-1938

The daughter of an unmarried laundress, Suzanne Valadon was a free spirit who wore a corsage of carrots, kept a goat at her studio to "eat up her bad drawings," and fed caviar to her "good Catholic" cats on Fridays.

Working as a model for artists like Toulouse-Lautrec and Jean Renoir, Valadon observed their techniques. Edgar Degas encouraged her efforts by purchasing her work and they became close friends. Best known for her candid female nudes, Valadon was such a perfectionist that she worked on some of her oil paintings for thirteen years before showing them. She became the first woman painter admitted to the Société Nationale des Beaux-Arts.

The cards laid out in *The Future Unveiled* could well be for divination through cartomancy. The card being read is a queen of diamonds, which represents a fair-haired woman, a flirt who loves to party and gossip.

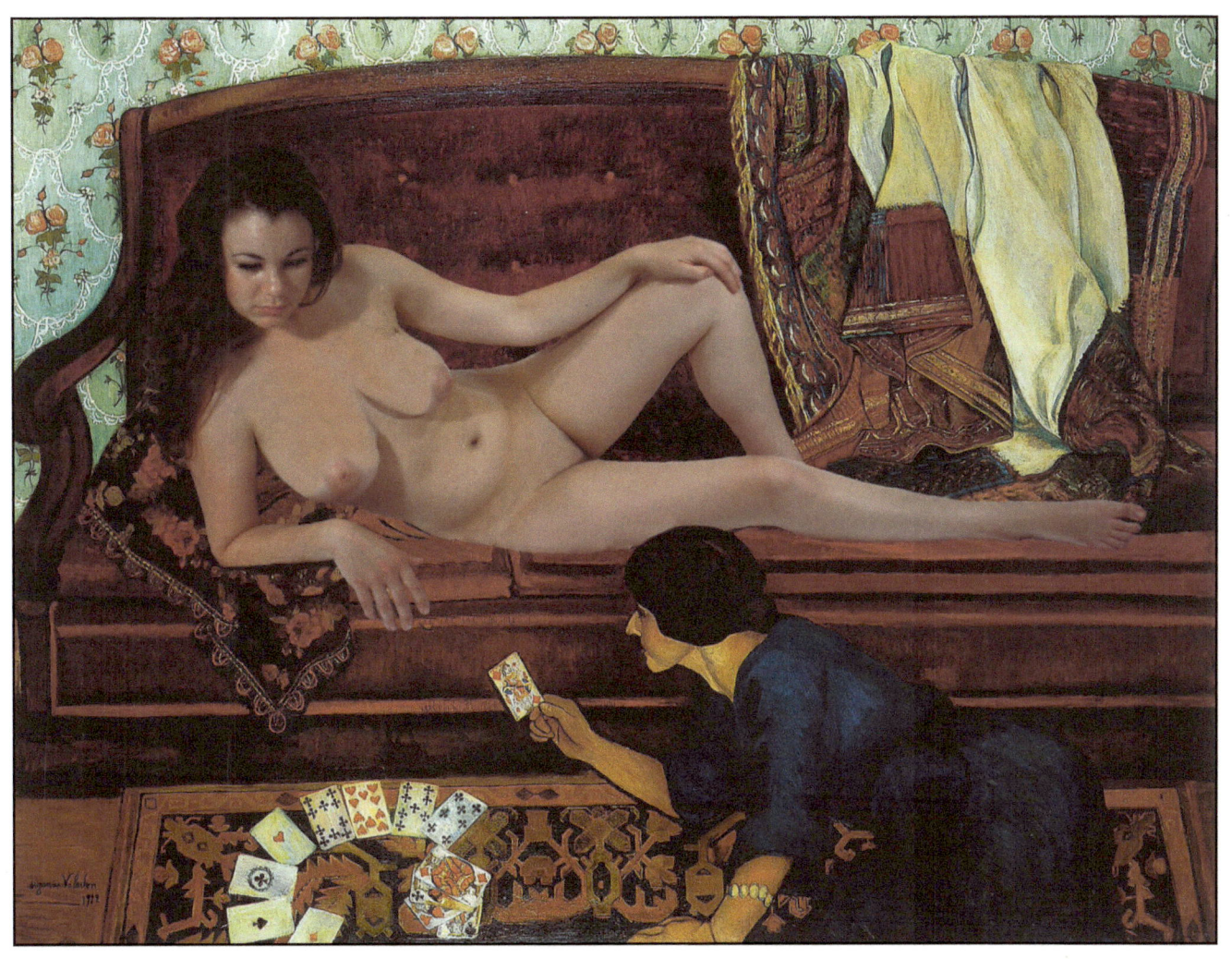

In the Cards

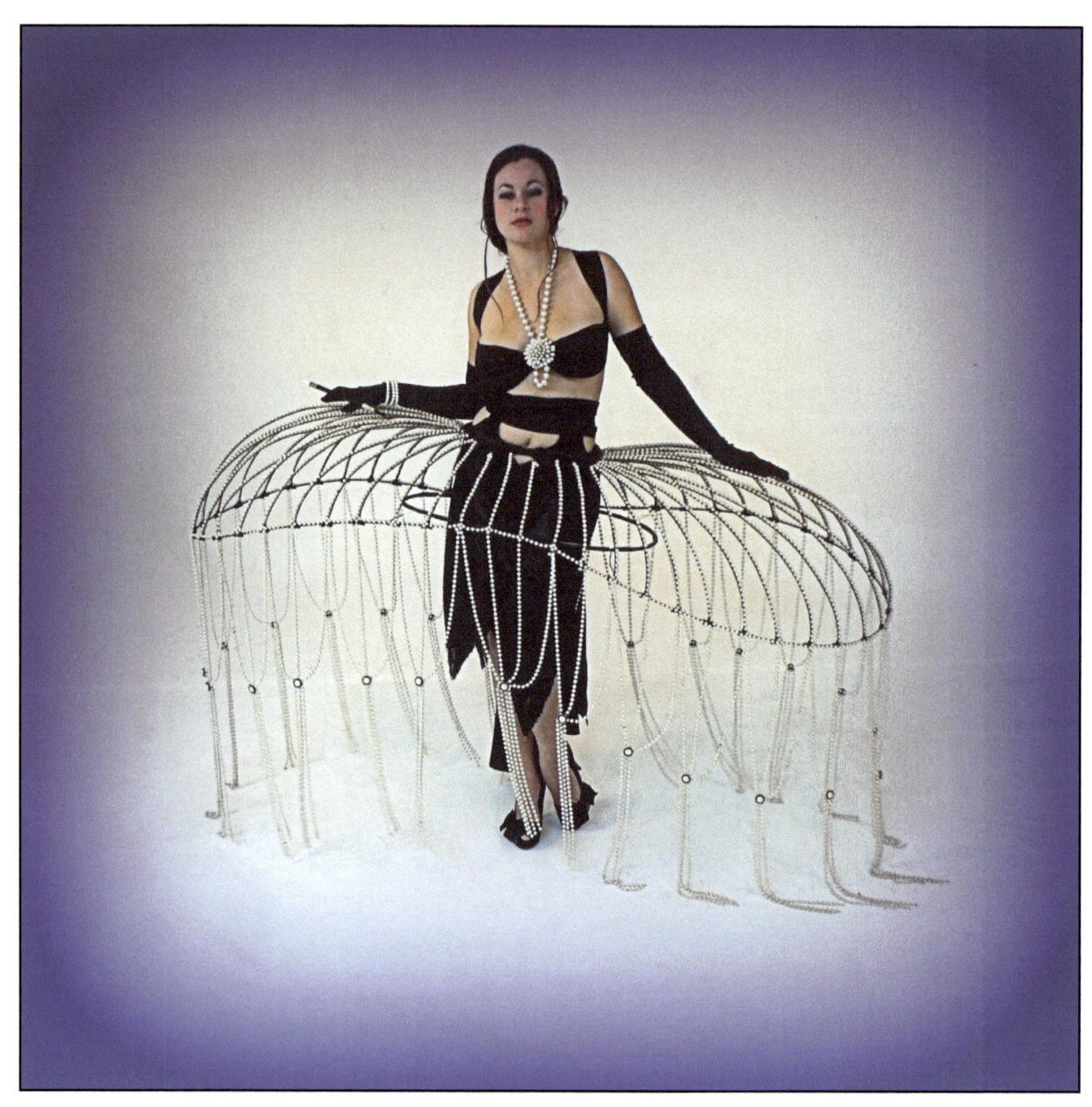

The Cage
Inspired by *Improvised Cage* in *Harper's Bazaar*, July, 1922
Erté, 1904-1989

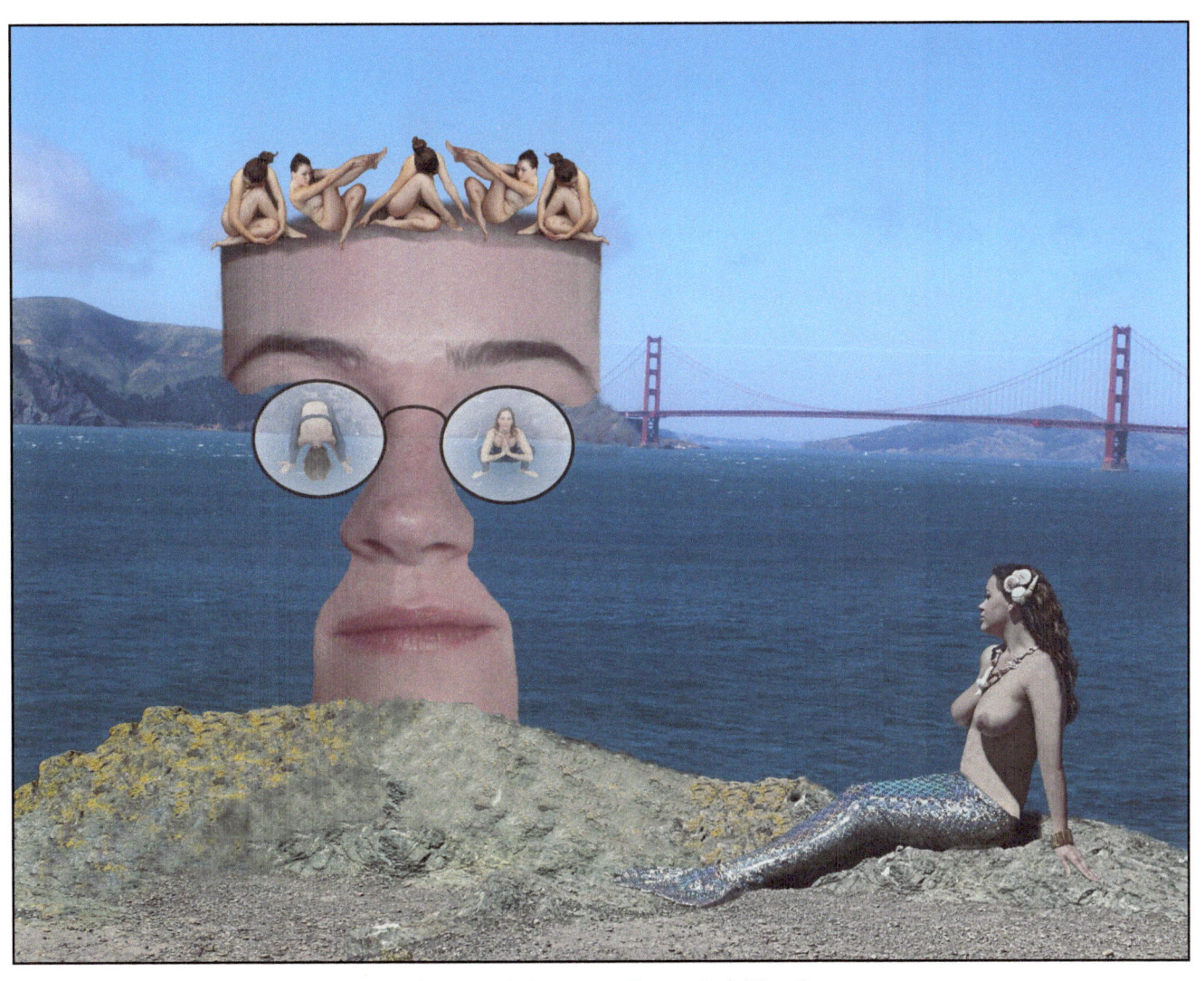

Apparition at Lands' End
Inspired by *Apparition of Face and Fruit Dish on a Beach*, 1938
Salvador Dali, 1904-1989

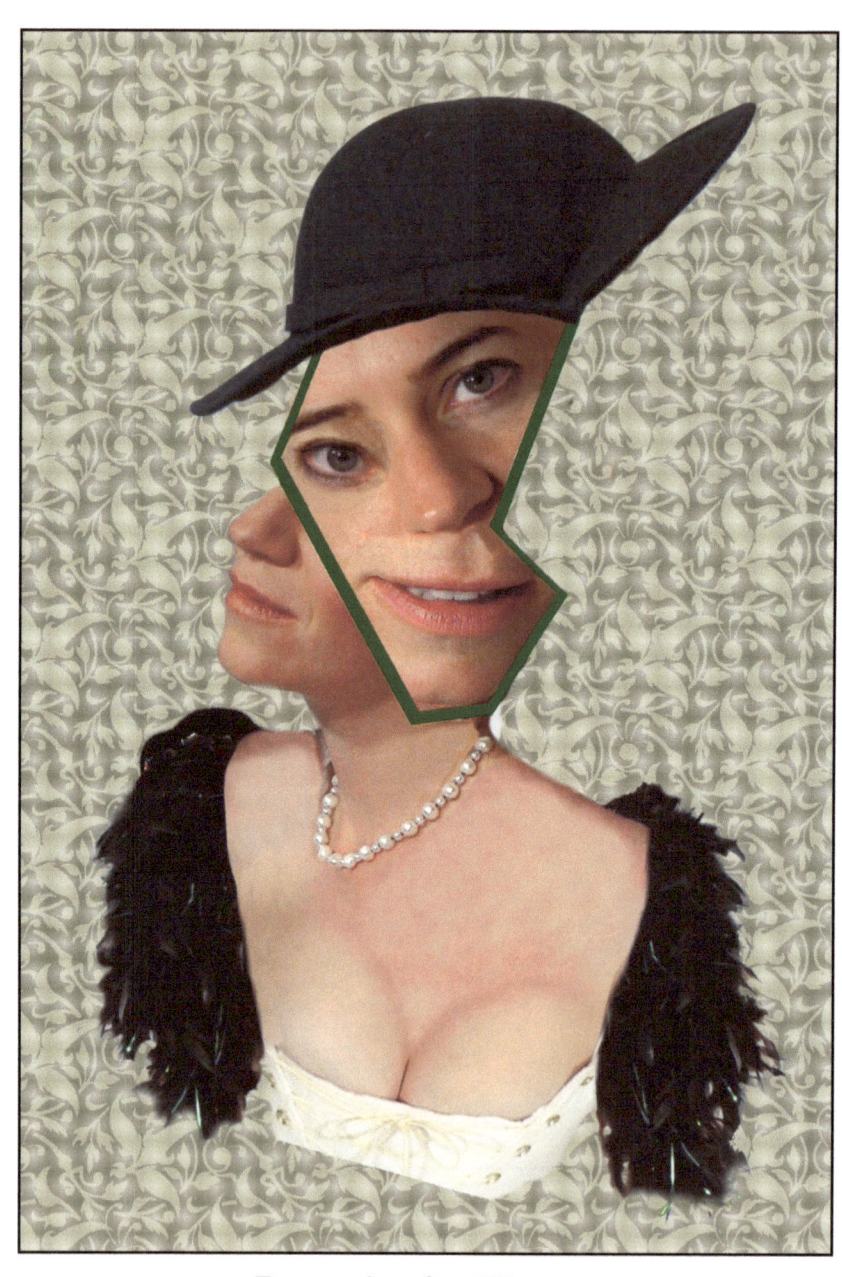

Portrait of a Woman
Inspired by *Bust of a Woman with a Hat*, 1939
Pablo Picasso, 1881-1973

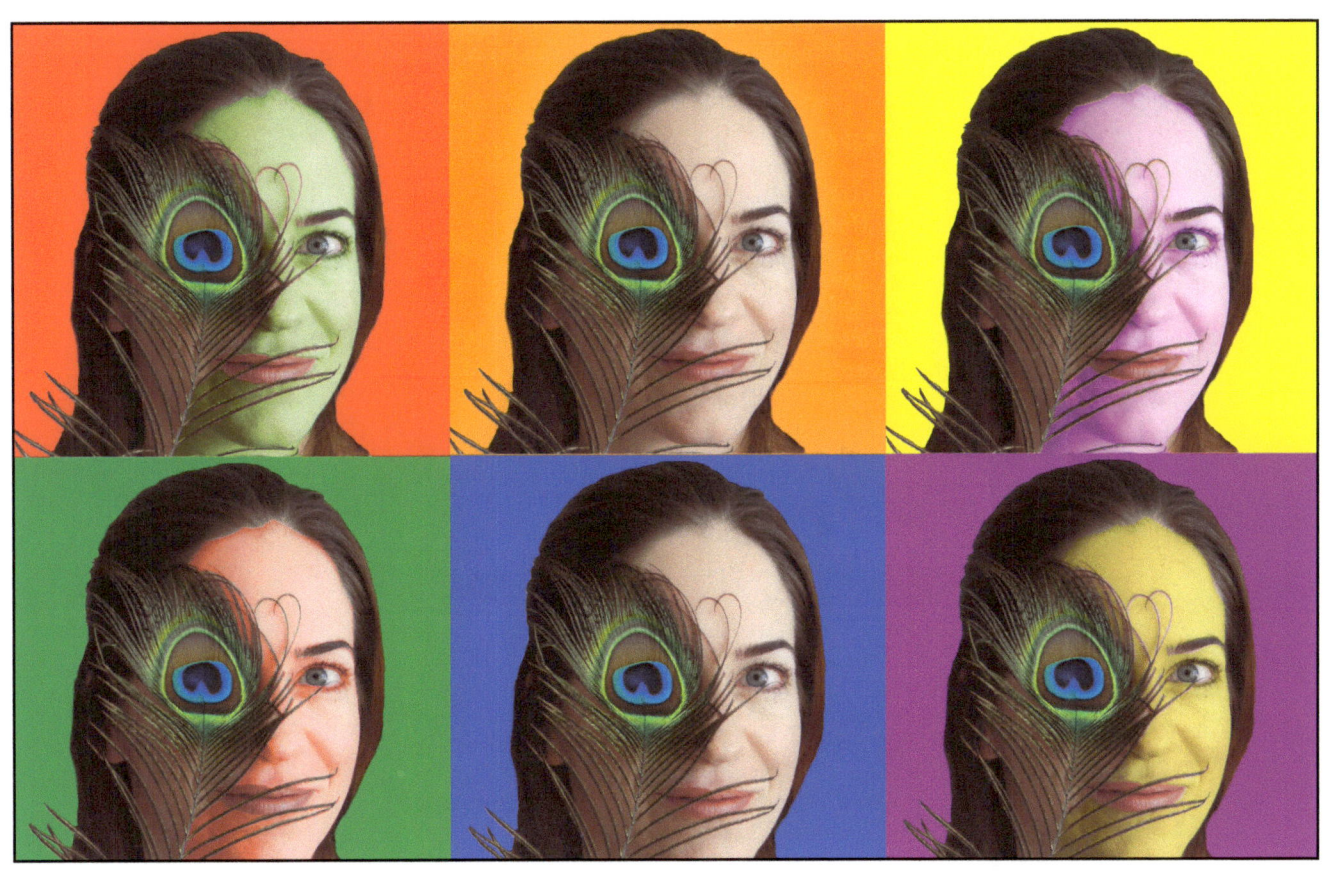

Peacock
Inspired by Andy Warhol's paintings of Marilyn Monroe in the 1960s

List of Sources

The images of classical art in this book are public domain images from Wikimedia.org or Wikipedia.org or royalty free images from Dover's Full-Color Design Series®.

Key: Com: = commons.wikimedia.org/wiki/File: Wiki: = en.wikipedia.org/wiki/File:

Akrotiri Papyrus Fresco
    Com: Akrotiri_papyrus.jpg
Amazonomachy Frieze
    Com: Amazonomachy_Halicarnassus_BM_n2.jpg
    Com: Amazonomachy_Halicarnassus_BM_1014.jpg
Birth of Venus, Sandro Botticelli
    #021 from *120 Italian Renaissance Paintings,* Dover Publications, Inc.
Cave of the Storm Nymphs, Edward Poynter
    #045 from *120 Great Victorian Fantasy Paintings,* Dover Publications, Inc.
Couple Waltzing, A, Eadweard Muybridge
    Wiki: Phenakistoscope_3g07690u.jpg
Crouching Woman, Auguste Rodin
    Com: Auguste_Rodin_001.jpg
Danaid, August Rodin
    Com: Auguste_Rodin_Danaiade_Gsell_29.jpg
David, Michelangelo
    Com: Replica_Michelangelo%27s_David_black_background.jpg
David and Goliath, Osmar Schindler
    Com: Osmar_Schindler_David_und_Goliath.jpg
Death of Marat, Jacques-Louis David
    Com: Death_of_Marat_by_David.jpg
Diana Bathing, Francois Boucher
    #011 from *120 Great Paintings of Nudes,* Dover Publications, Inc.
Dream, The, Henri Rousseau
    #094 from *120 Great Paintings of Nudes,* Dover Publications, Inc.
Echo and Narcissus, John William Waterhouse
    #114 from *120 Great Victorian Fantasy Paintings,* Dover Publications, Inc.
Future Unveiled, The, Suzanne Valadon
    #108 from *120 Great Paintings of Nudes,* Dover Publications, Inc.
Glade, The, Julius LeBlanc Stewart
    #102 from *120 Great Paintings of Nudes,* Dover Publications, Inc.
Heptu Bidding Farewell to the City of Obb, John Duncan
    #045 from *120 Great Victorian Fantasy Paintings,* Dover Publications, Inc.
Hope in the Prison of Despair, Evelyn de Morgan
    #057 from *120 Great Victorian Fantasy Paintings,* Dover Publications, Inc.
Judgment of Paris, 1512-14, Lucas Cranach the Elder
    Com: Lucas_Cranach_d._%C3%84._-_The_Judgment_of_Paris_-_WGA05629.jpg
Judgment of Paris, 1528, Lucas Cranach the Elder
    Com: The_Judgment_of_Paris.jpg

Judgment of Paris, 1530, Lucas Cranach the Elder
    Com: Lucas_Cranach_the_Elder_-_Judgment_of_Paris.jpg
La Fornarina, Raphael
    Com: Raffael_045.jpg
Large Odalisque, Jean-August-Dominique Ingres
    #051 from *120 Great Paintings of Nudes*, Dover Publications, Inc.
Luncheon on the Grass, Édouard Manet
    #065 from *120 Great Paintings of Nudes*, Dover Publications, Inc.
Mermaid, A, John William Waterhouse
    #112 from 120 *Great Victorian Fantasy Paintings*, Dover Publications, Inc.
Minoan Snake Goddess
    Photo by author
Models, Georges Seurat
    #100 from *120 Great Paintings of Nudes*, Dover Publications, Inc.
Ophelia, John Everett Millais
    #078 from *120 Great Paintings*, Dover Publications, Inc.
Painter's Studio, Gustave Courbet
    Com: Courbet,_Gustave_-_The_Painter%27s_Studio_-1855.jpg
Scream, The, Edvard Munch
    #084 from *120 Great Paintings*, Dover Publications, Inc.
Spirit of the Night, John Atkinson Grimshaw
    #056 from *120 Great Victorian Fantasy Paintings*, Dover Publications, Inc.
Thorn Puller
    Com: Spinario_BM_1755.jpg (photographer: Jastrow)
Venus and Cupid, Diego Velazquez
    #113 from *120 Great Paintings of Nudes*, Dover Publications, Inc.
Venus de Milo, Alexandros of Antioch
    Com: Venus_de_Milo_Louvre_Ma399.jpg
Woman in the Bath, Edgar Degas
    Wiki: Edgar_Germain_Hilaire_Degas_032.jpg

Quotes:
Edvard Munch: "I was walking along a path..."
    "Quick Facts." *Becoming Edvard Munch*. The Art Institute of Chicago.
Gustave Courbet: "When I am dead..."
    Courbet, Gustave: *Letters of Gustave Courbet*, 1992, University of Chicago Press
Evelyn de Morgan: "Art is eternal, but life is short..."
    Smith, Elise (2002). *Evelyn Pickering De Morgan and the Allegorical Body*.
    Madison, NJ: Fairleigh Dickinson University Press.
Willem de Kooning: "None of us would have existed without him."
    Schneider, Pierre, "Through the Louvre with Barnett Newman,"
    ARTnews (June 1969)
Ingres: "Draw lines young man,..."
    Werner, Alfred. *Degas Pastels*. New York: Watson-Guptill.
Rousseau: "When I go into the glass houses..."
    http://en.wikipedia.org/wiki/Henri_Rousseau

Index

www.ingramcontent.com/pod-product-compliance
Lightning Source LLC
Chambersburg PA
CBHW050753180526
45159CB00003B/1445